Drawn by Jane Levi
&
Colored by Laety' Esperanza

"Global Doodle Gems"
Mini Collection Volume 1

Drawn
&
Colored
by
DomDomx

Drawn
&
Colored
by
Lynne McGee

Drawn & Colored by Yaya

50 Wonderful Designs

to color

from 16 awesome artists......

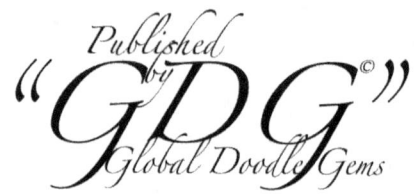

Copyright © 2015 Global Doodle Gems
Published by Global Doodle Gems
                Anna-Marie Vibeke Wedel

All rights are reserved by Global Doodle Gems.

Duplication of pages for personal use are allowed.  You are invited to color the pages then scan/post your coloured versions to social networks, mentioning the book title and author/artist (Global Doodle Gems).

All artwork and images are protected by copyright laws.  This book or any portion thereof may not, otherwise, be reproduced and/or distributed or transmitted without the express written permission of the artist/publisher of Global Doodle Gems.

All of us from the Global Doodle Gems wish you a colortastic time and look forward to seeing your wonderful color results online !

Contributing Artists to the first miniedition of "Global Doodle Gems"
Thank you for your contributions

Lynne McGee, Creative Rosalien, Velvet Comeay, Tammy Stansbery, Diane Holmes, Joseph Shivery, Linda Karpinski, Yaya, Nancy Sutton Lewin, Lynni Ex, Jane Levi, DomDomx, Dianne Comeau, Johanna Ans, Iben Lykke Højholdt
and
Bev Choy

*Contributing Artist*
*Lynne McGee*
*Brisbane, Australia*

Facebook : Colorandtangle

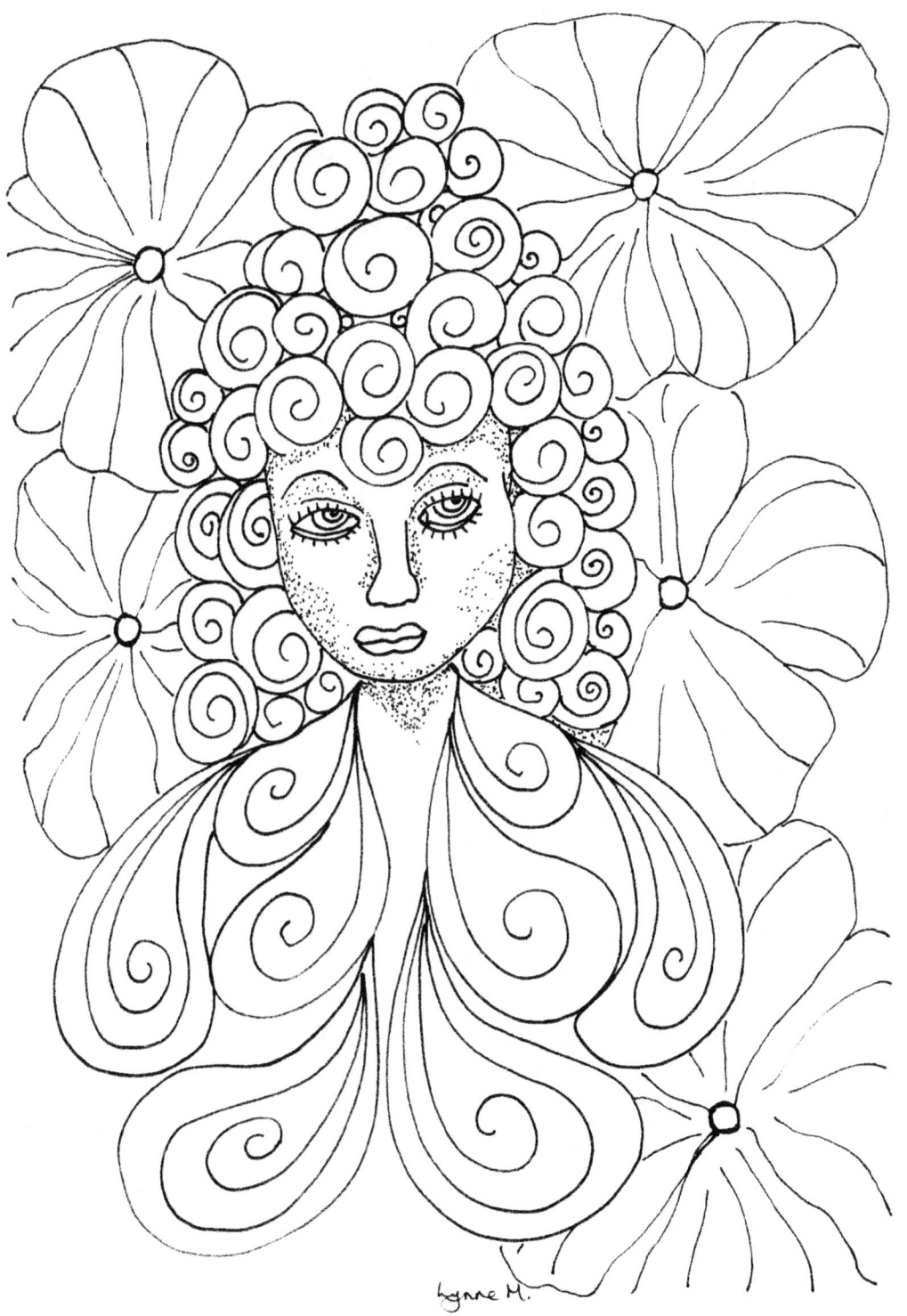

*Contributing Artist
Lynne McGee
Brisbane, Australia*

Facebook : Colorandtangle

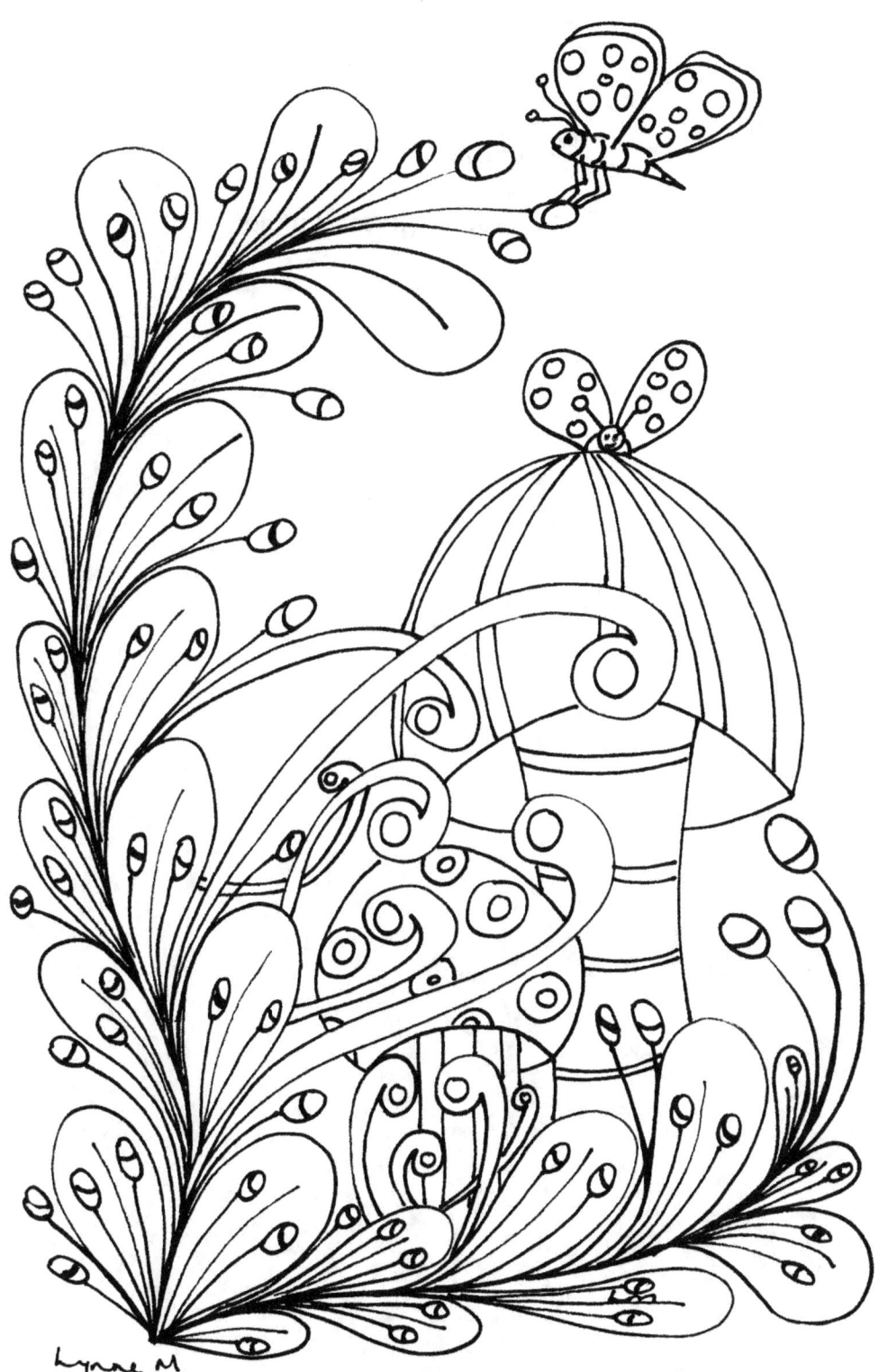

*Contributing Artist*
*Lynne McGee*
*Brisbane, Australia*

Facebook : Colorandtangle

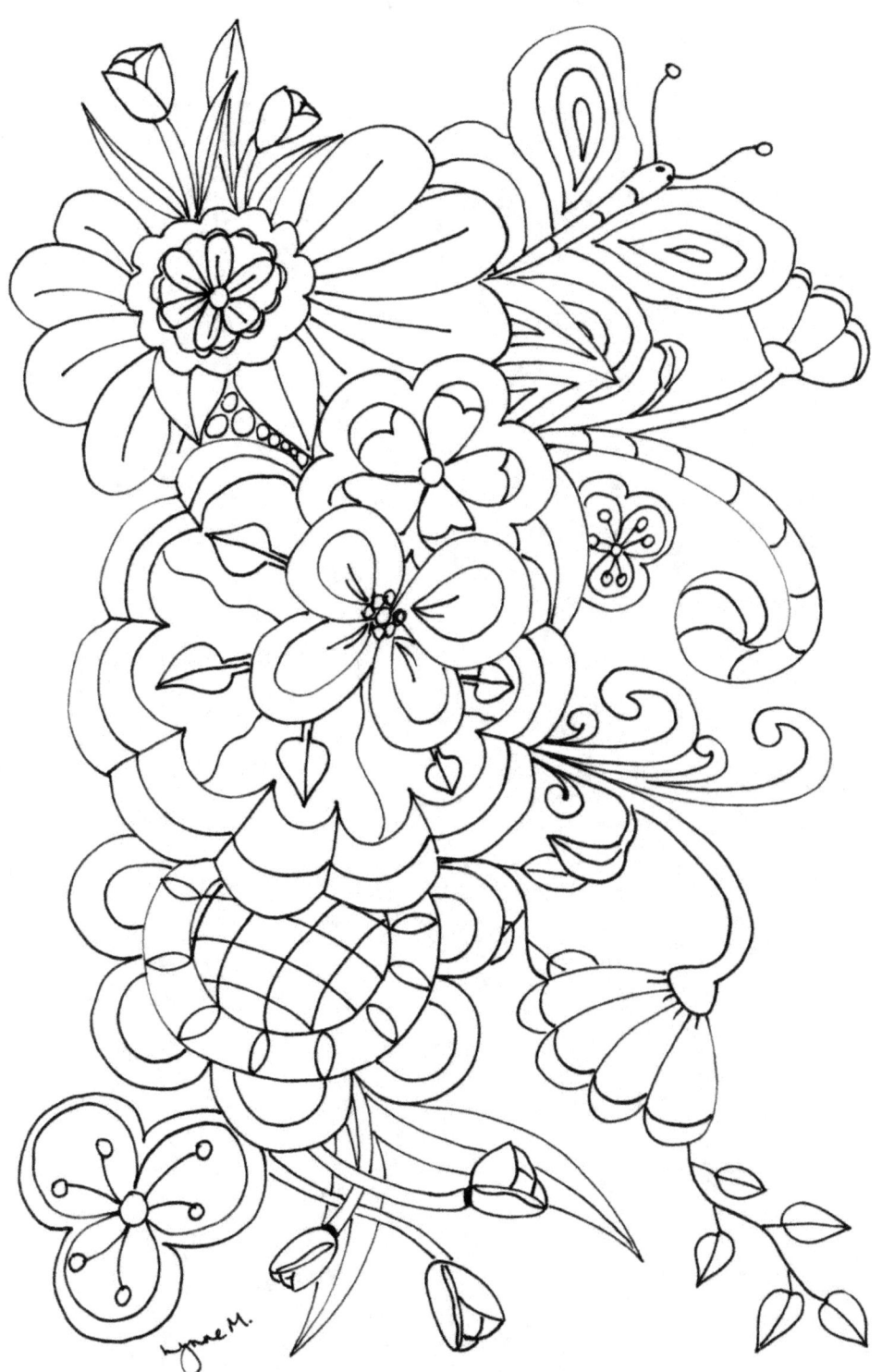

*Contributing Artist
Lynne McGee
Brisbane, Australia*

Facebook : Colorandtangle

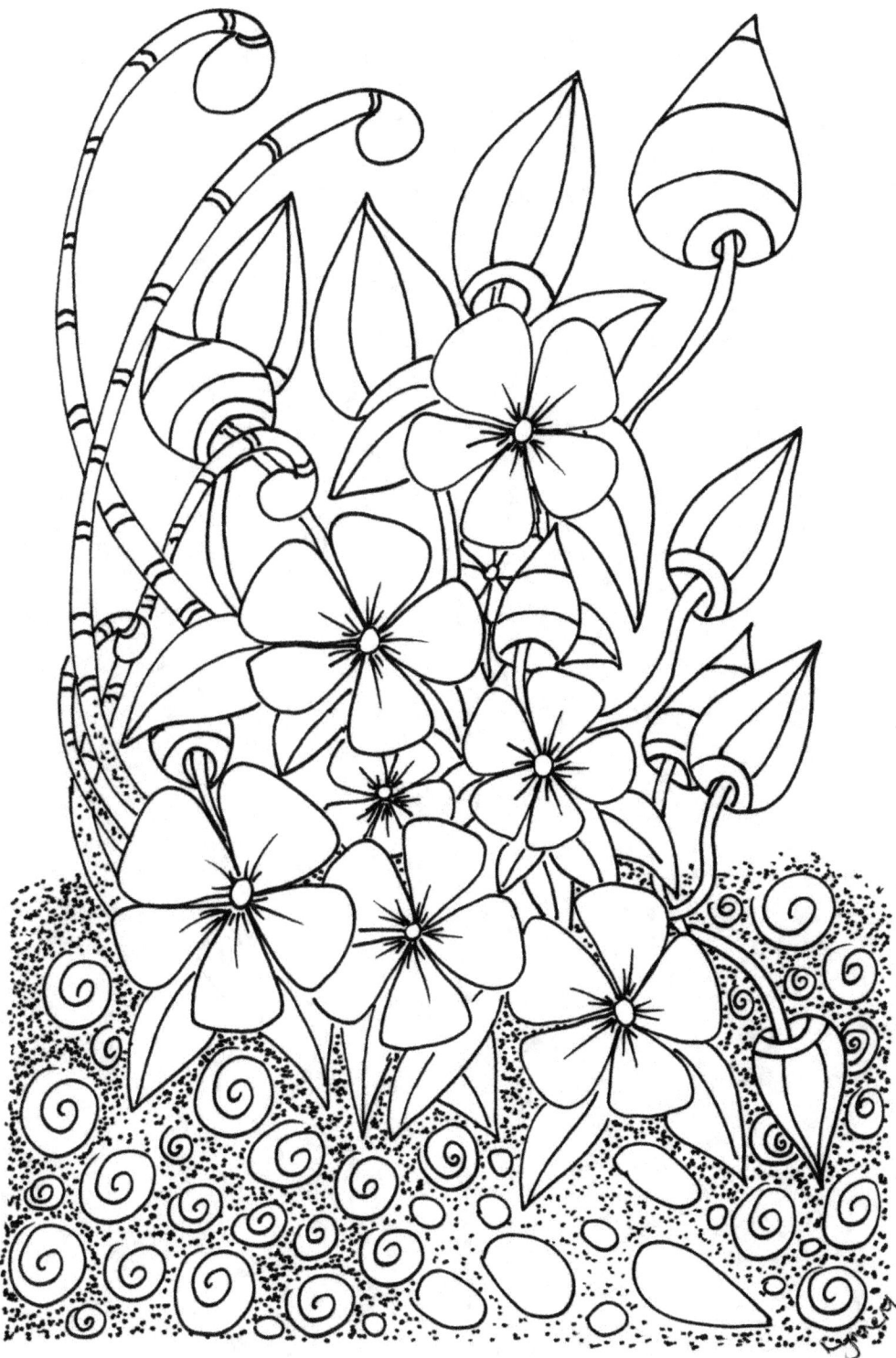

*Contributing Artist*
*Creative Rosalien*
*Norway*

Facebook : Creative Rosalien

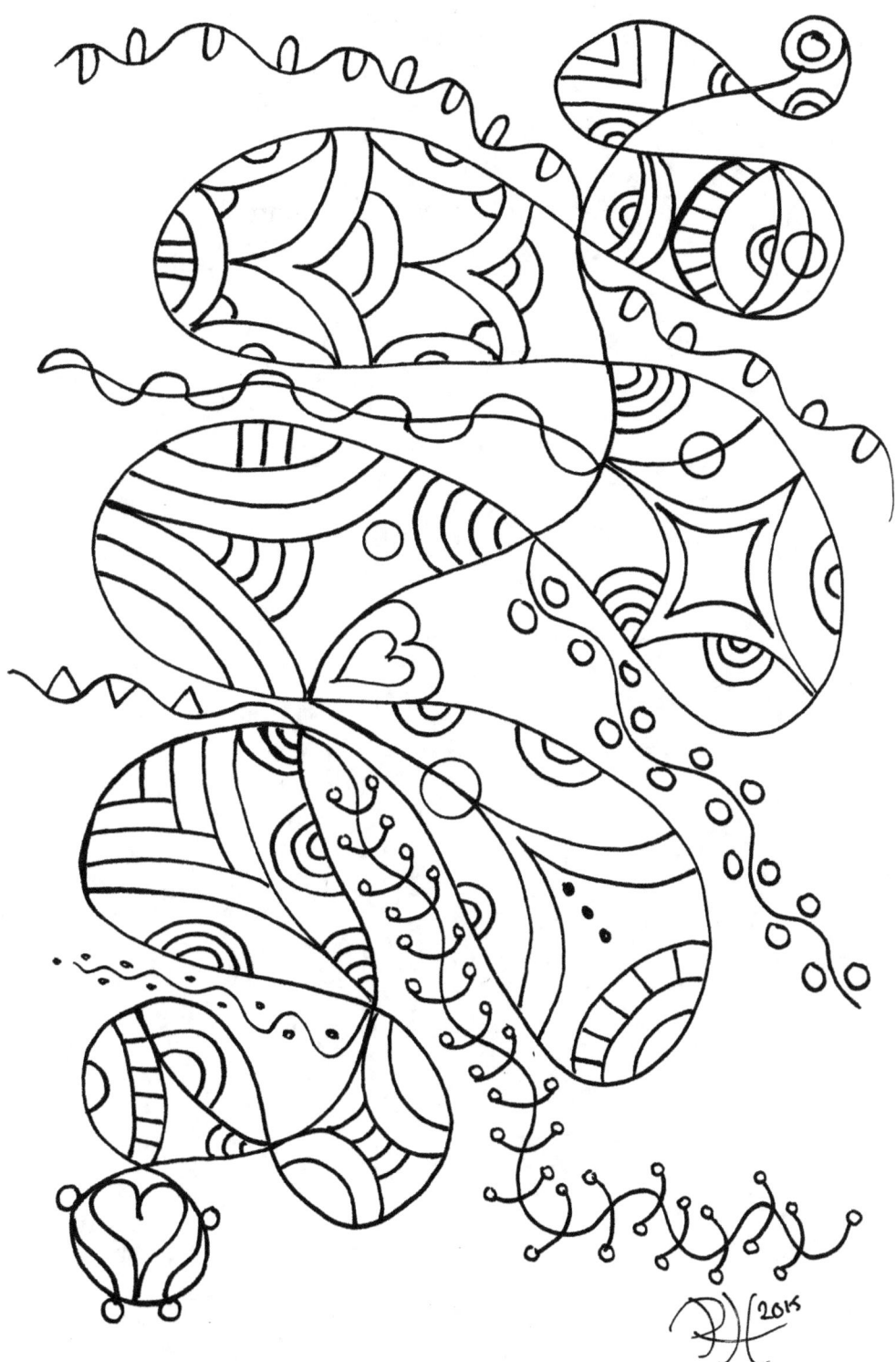

*Contributing Artist*
*Velvet Comeau*
*Canada*

Facebook : tranquilmoonart

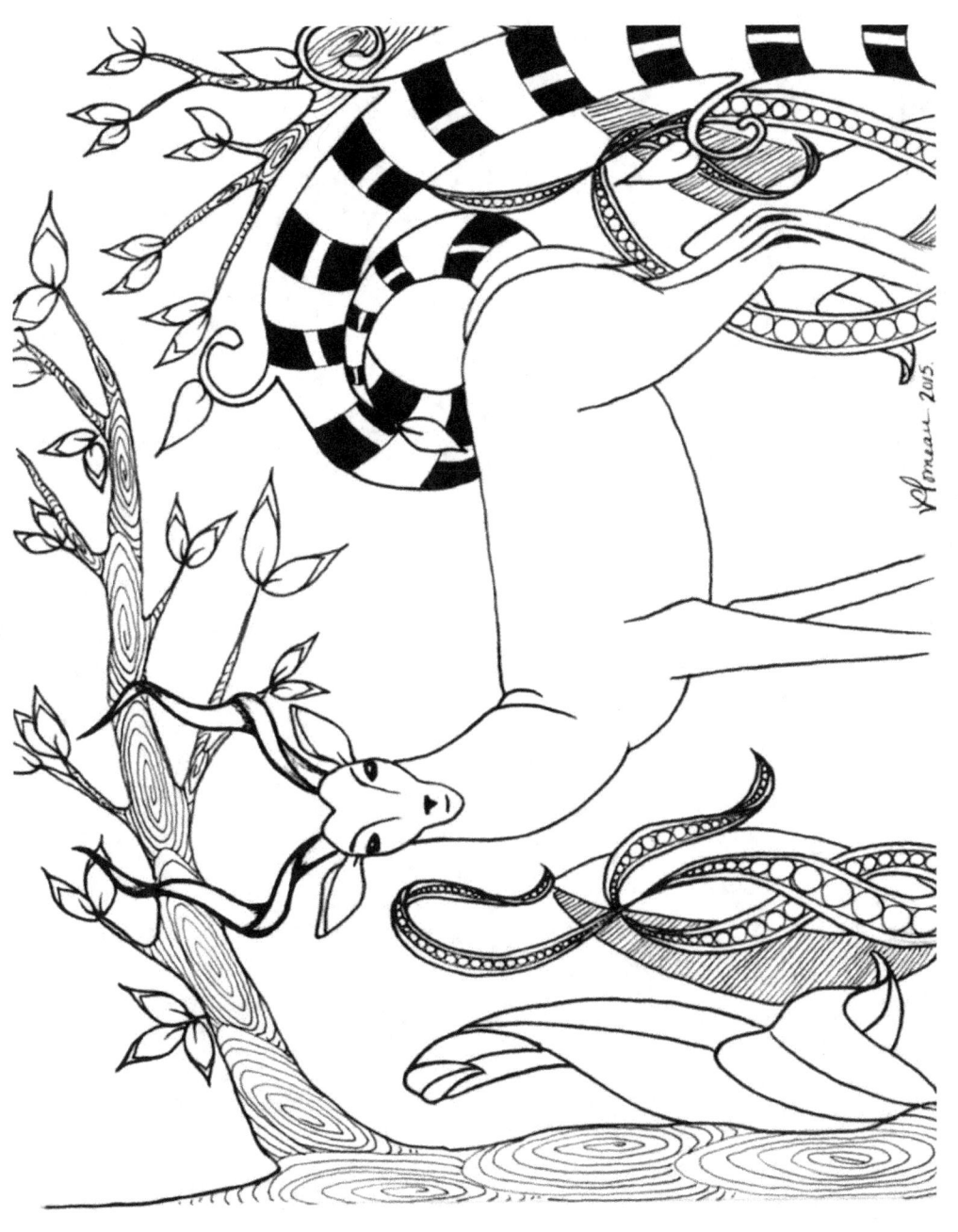

*Contributing Artist*
*Tammy Stansbery*
*USA*

Facebook : TJsArtCorner

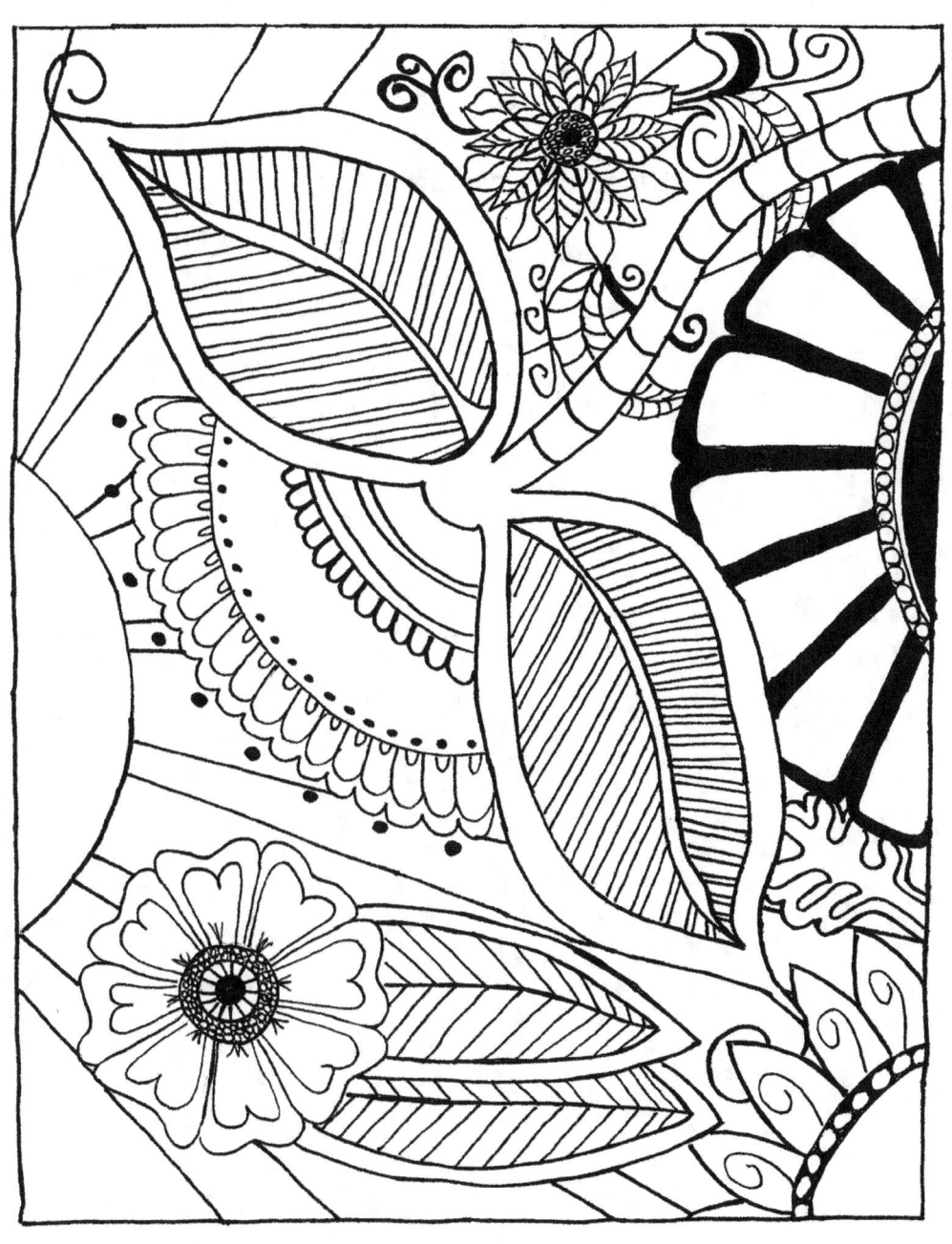

*Contributing Artist*
*Diana Holmes*
*USA*

Facebook : WhimsicalCheers

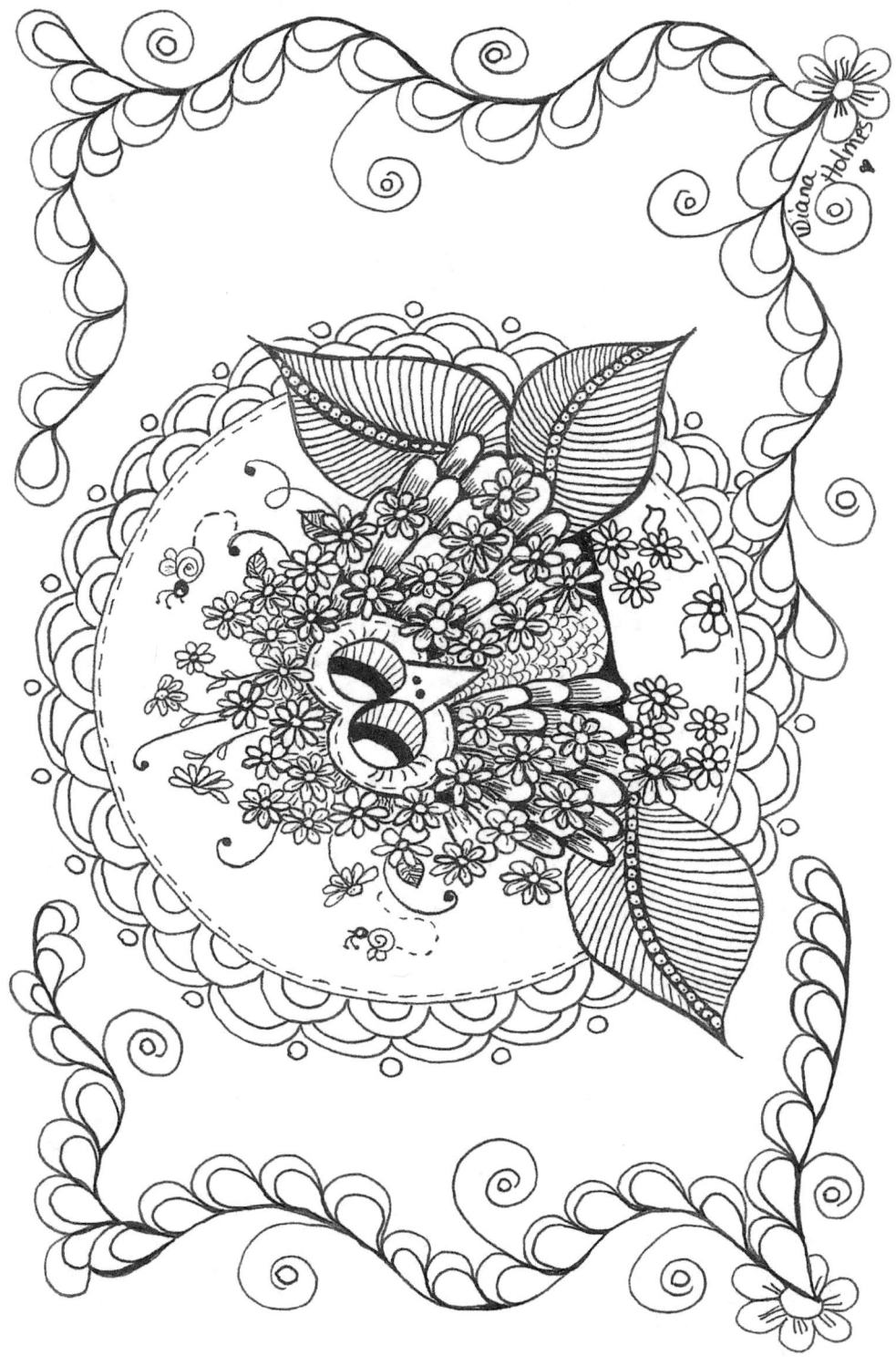

*Contributing Artist*
*Diana Holmes*
*USA*

Facebook : WhimsicalCheers

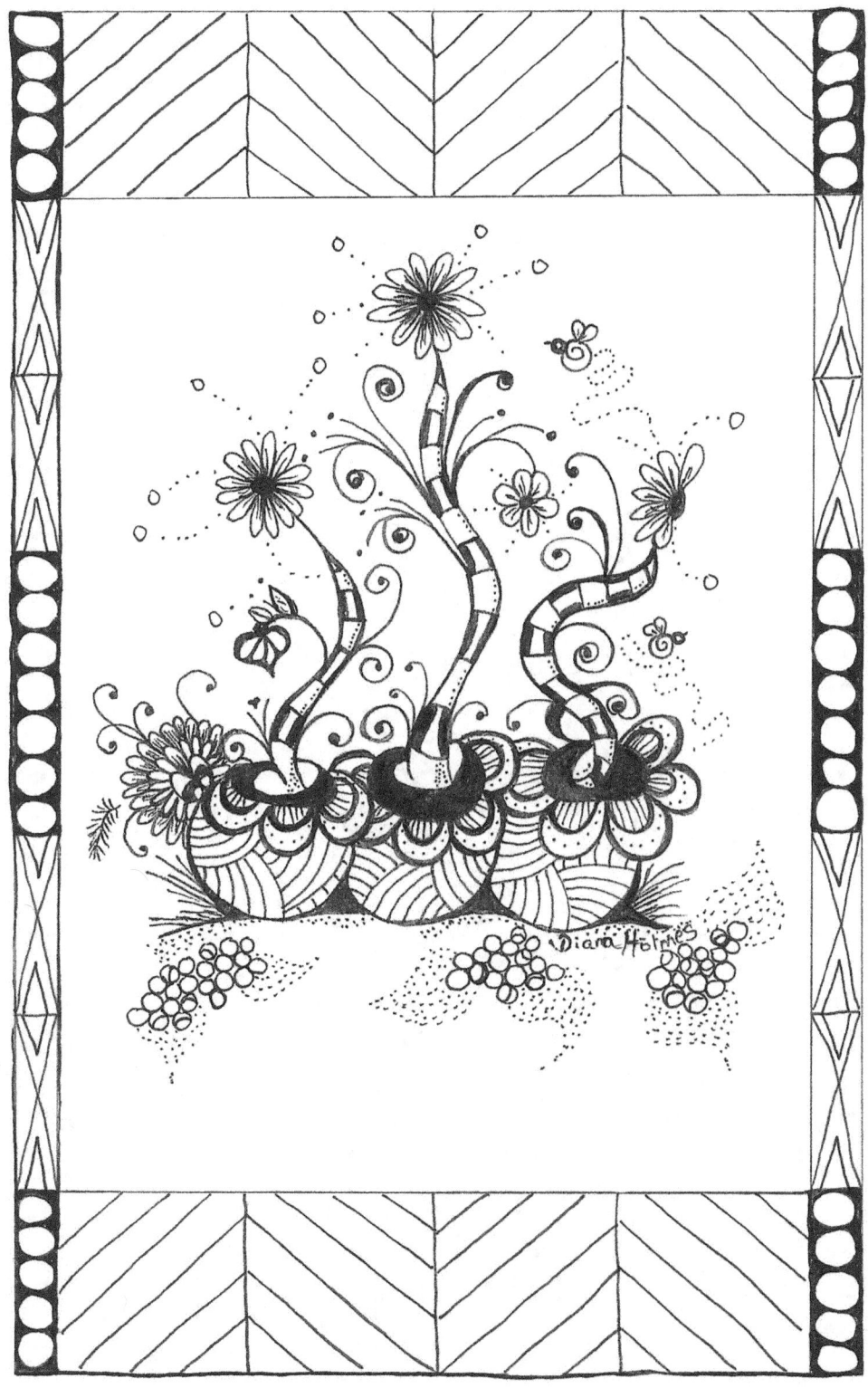

*Contributing Artist*
*Velvet Comeau*
*Canada*

Facebook : tranquilmoonart

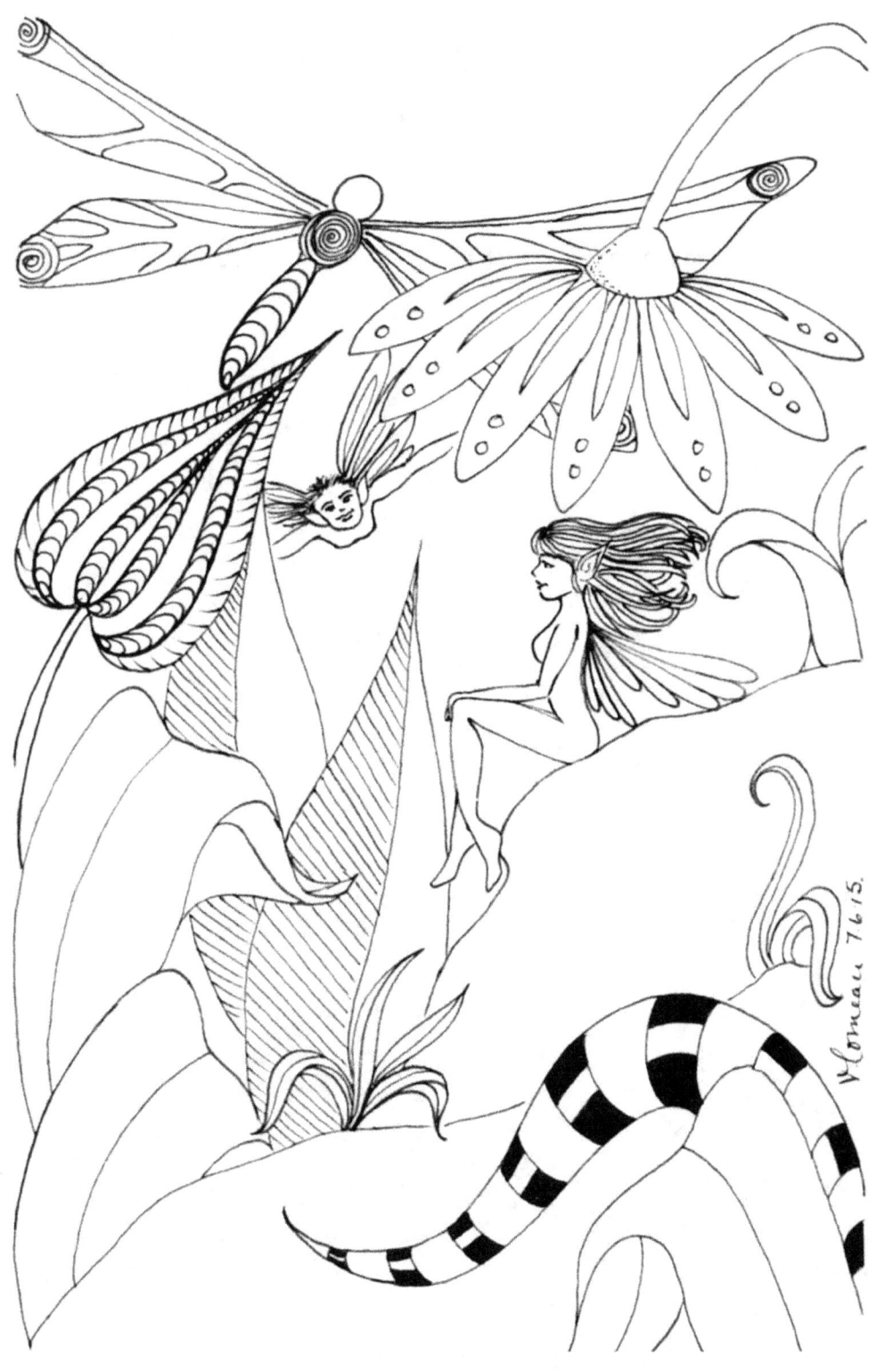

*Contributing Artist*
*Joseph Shivery*
*USA*

Facebook : The-Broken-Mind-of-Joes-Ink

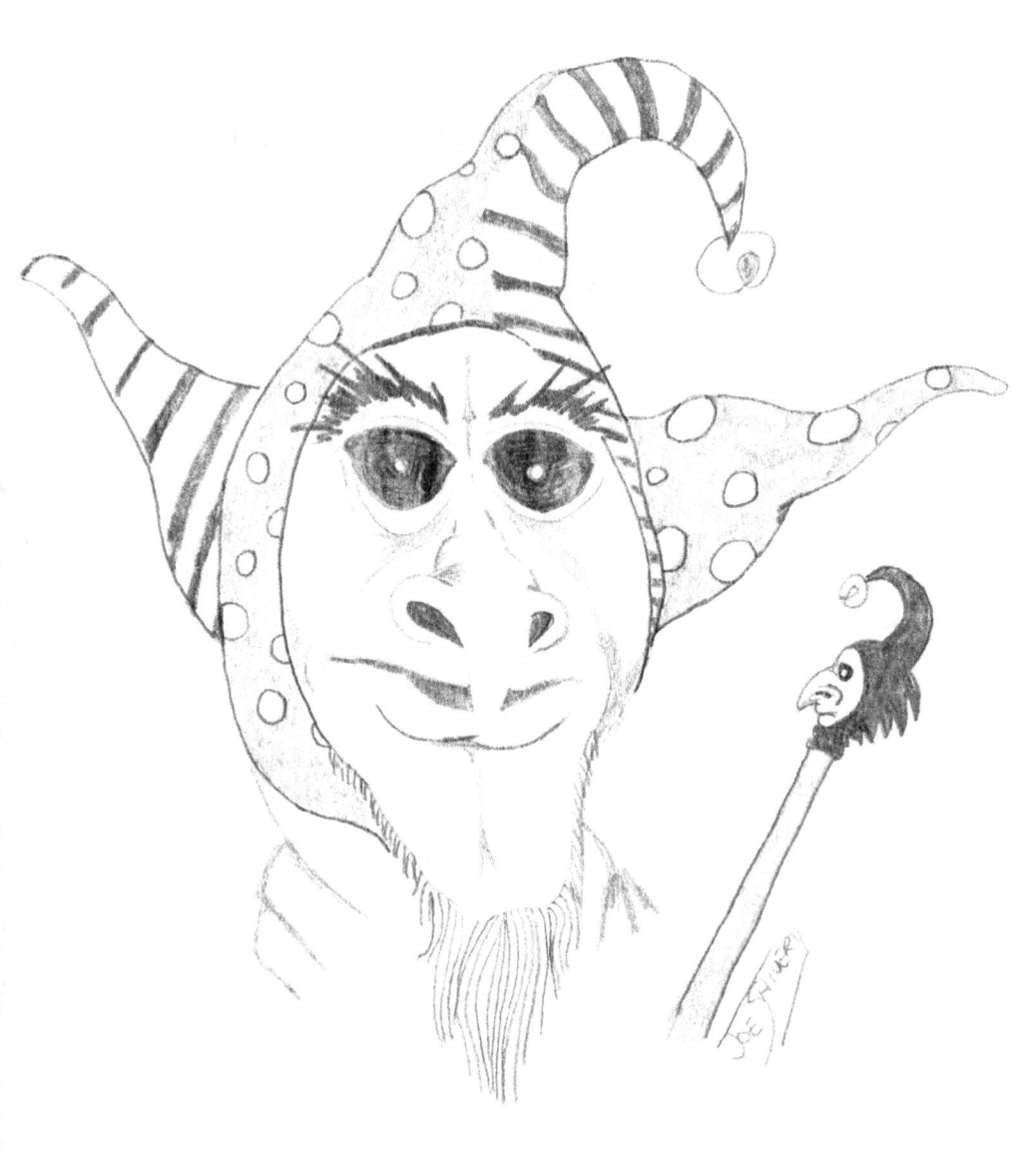

*Contributing Artist*
*Joseph Shivery*
*USA*

Facebook : The-Broken-Mind-of-Joes-Ink

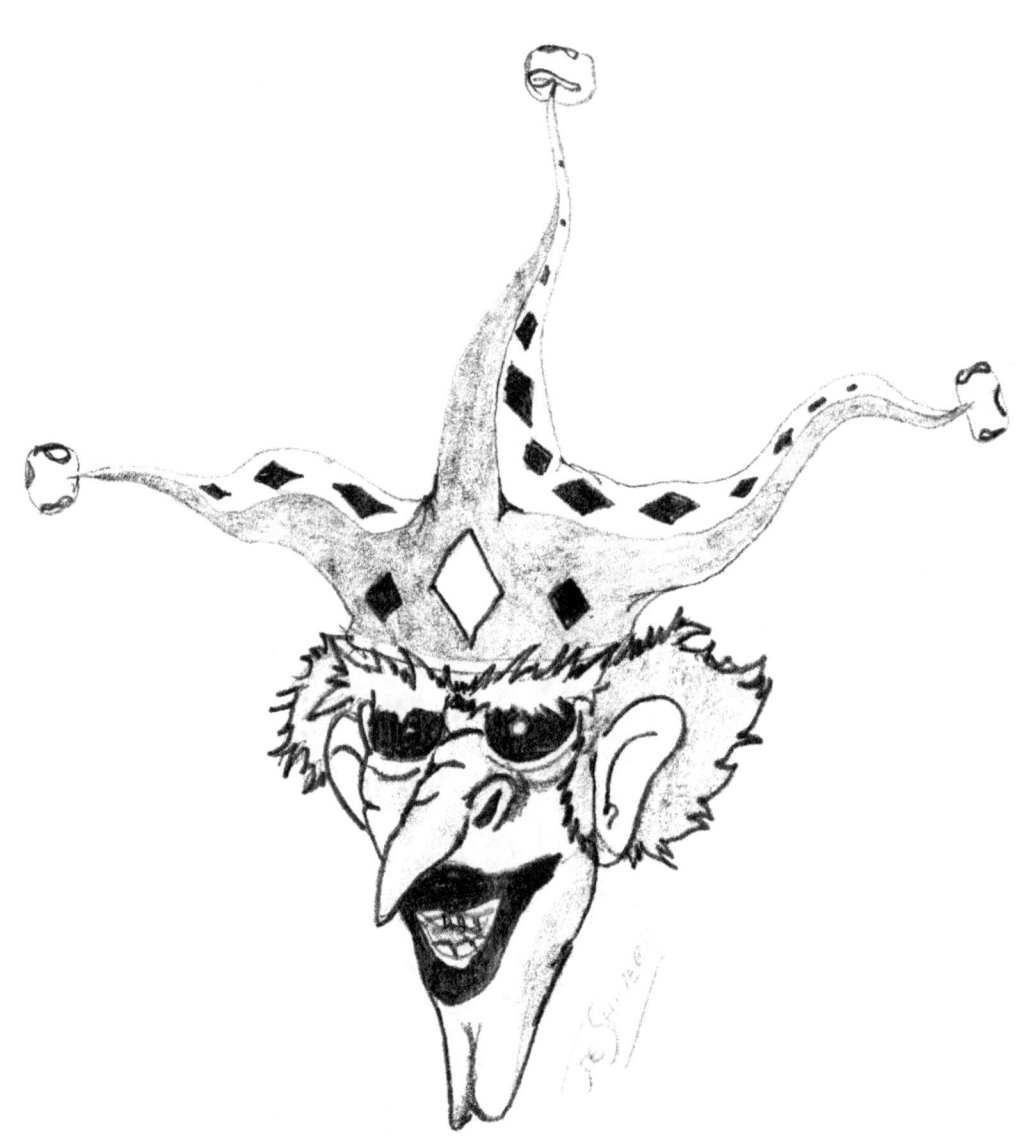

*Contributing Artist*
*Joseph Shivery*
*USA*

Facebook : The-Broken-Mind-of-Joes-Ink

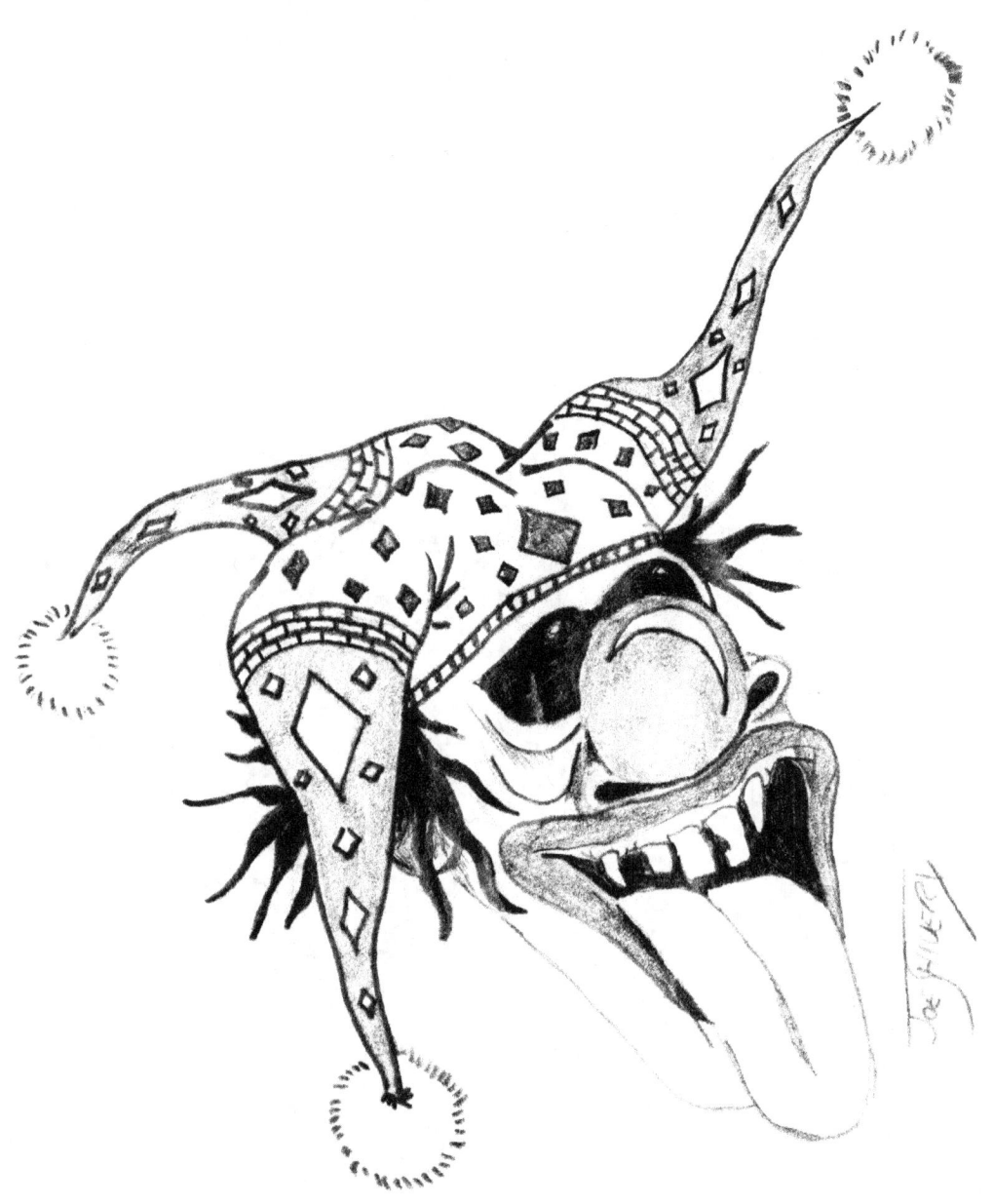

*Contributing Artist*
*Joseph Shivery*
*USA*

Facebook : The-Broken-Mind-of-Joes-Ink

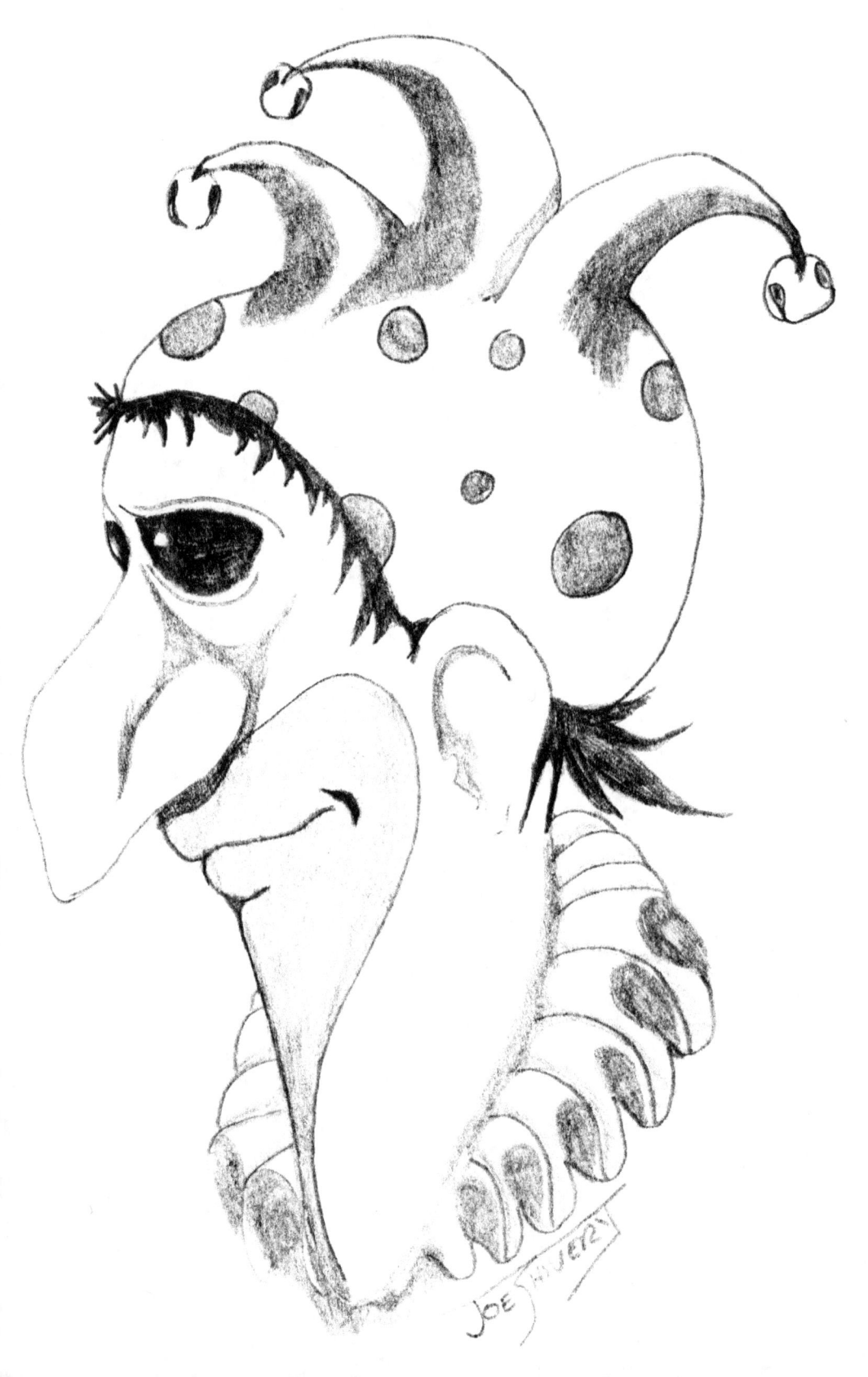

*Contributing Artist*
*Joseph Shivery*
*USA*

Facebook : The-Broken-Mind-of-Joes-Ink

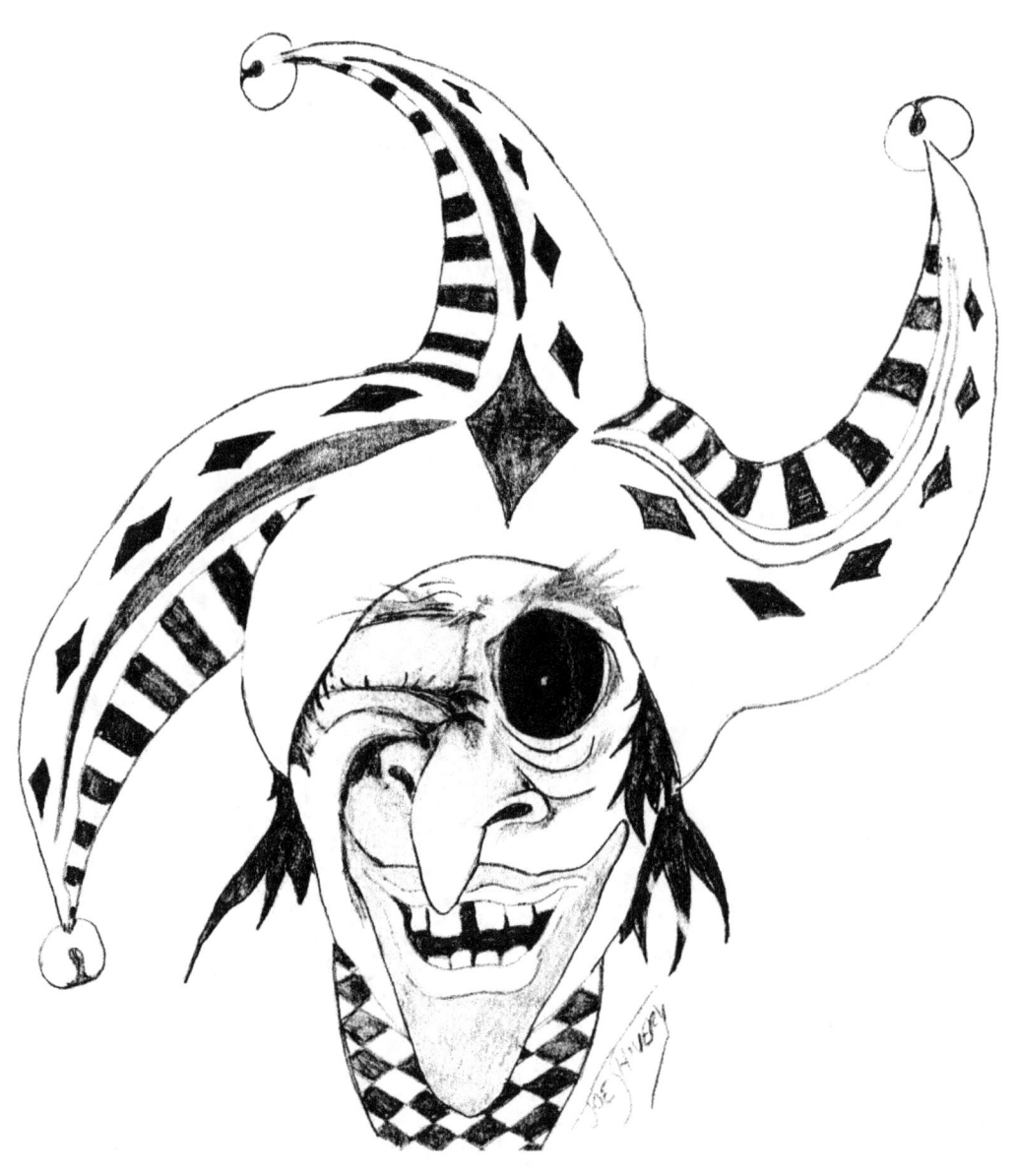

*Contributing Artist*
*Linda Karpinski*
*USA*

Facebook : Blue-Monkey-Kreations_Art-Page

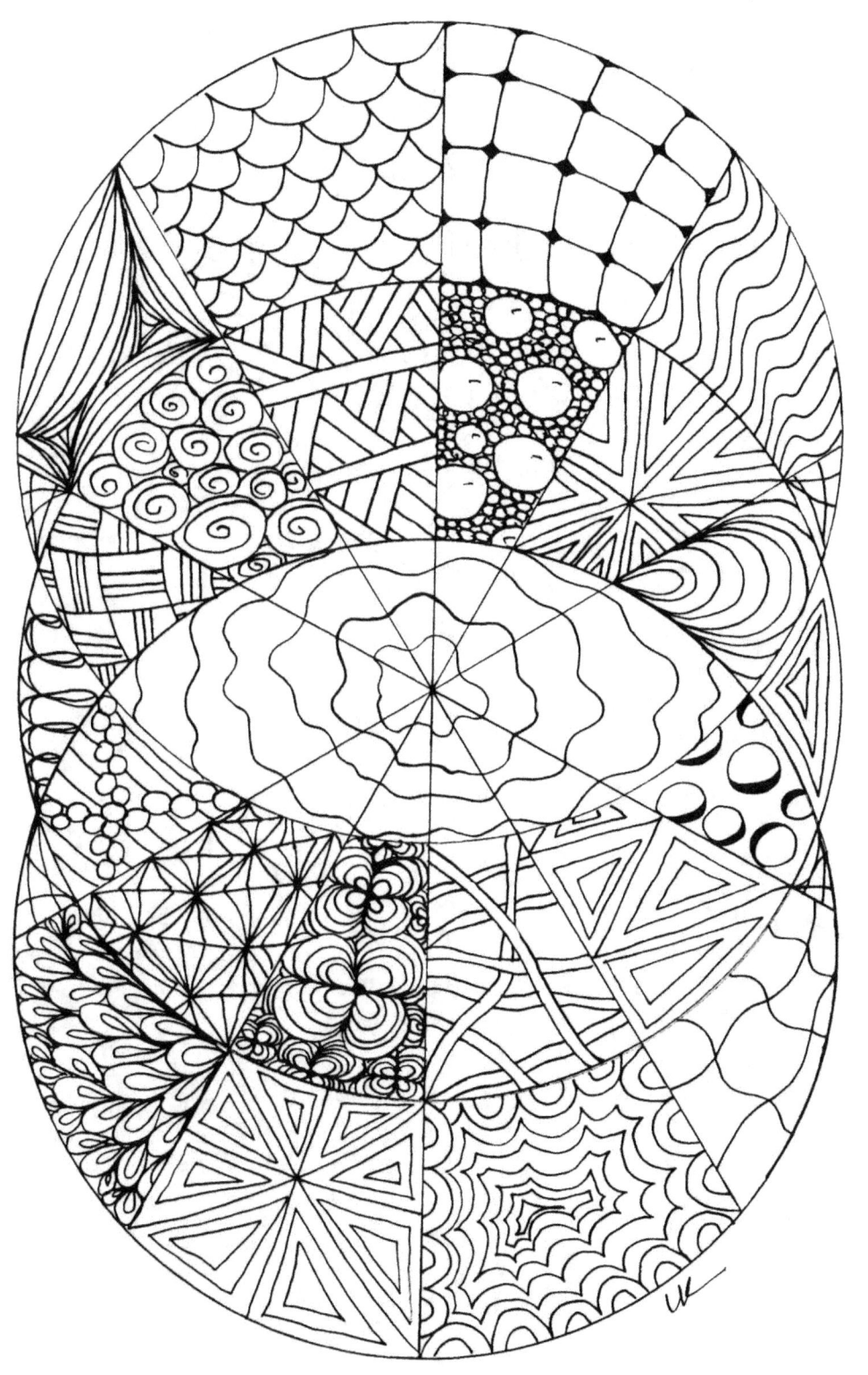

*Contributing Artist*
*Yaya*
*France*

Facebook : Les-gribouillis-de-yaya-georgia-merino

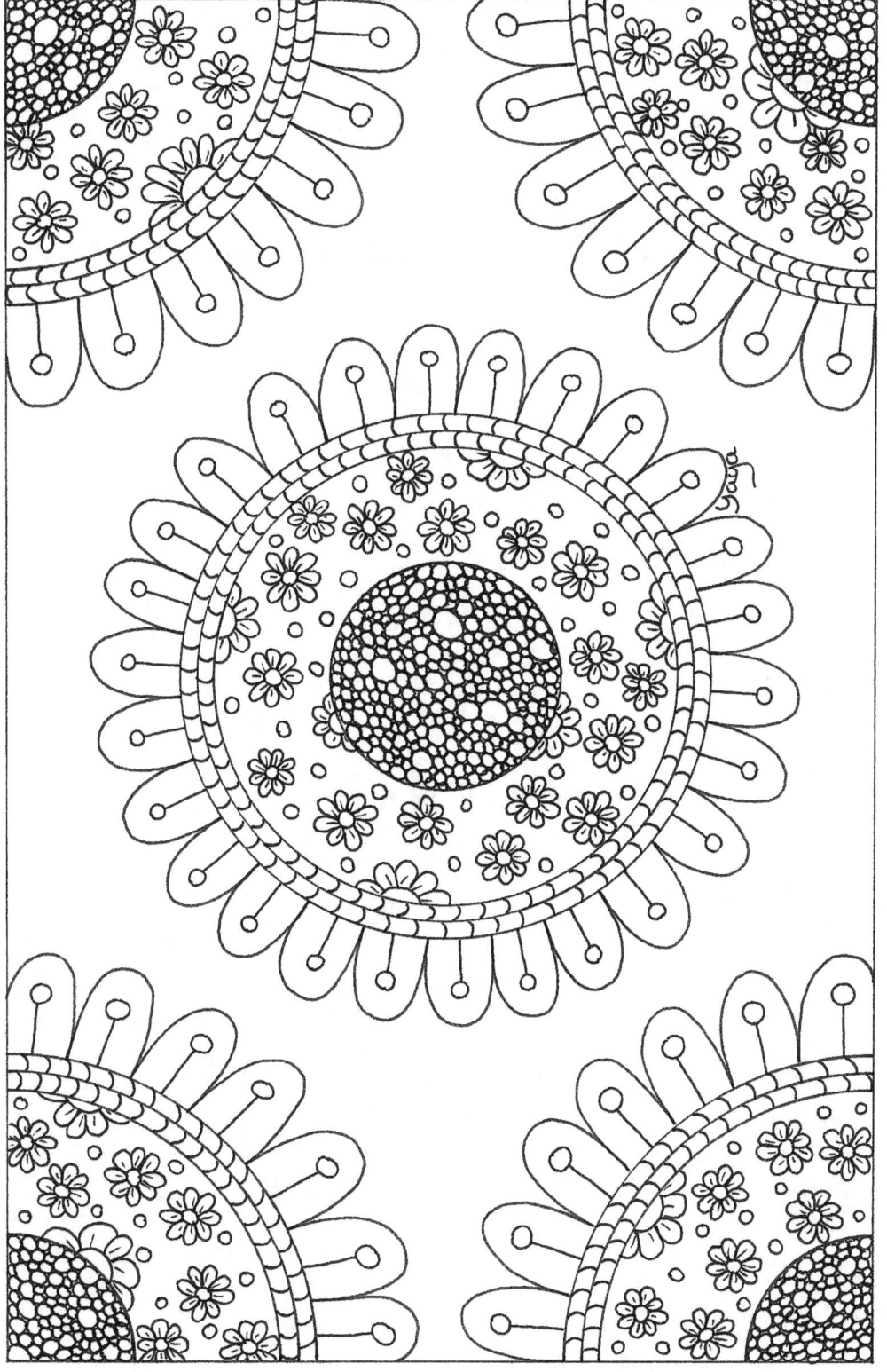

*Contributing Artist*
*Yaya*
*France*

Facebook : Les-gribouillis-de-yaya-georgia-merino

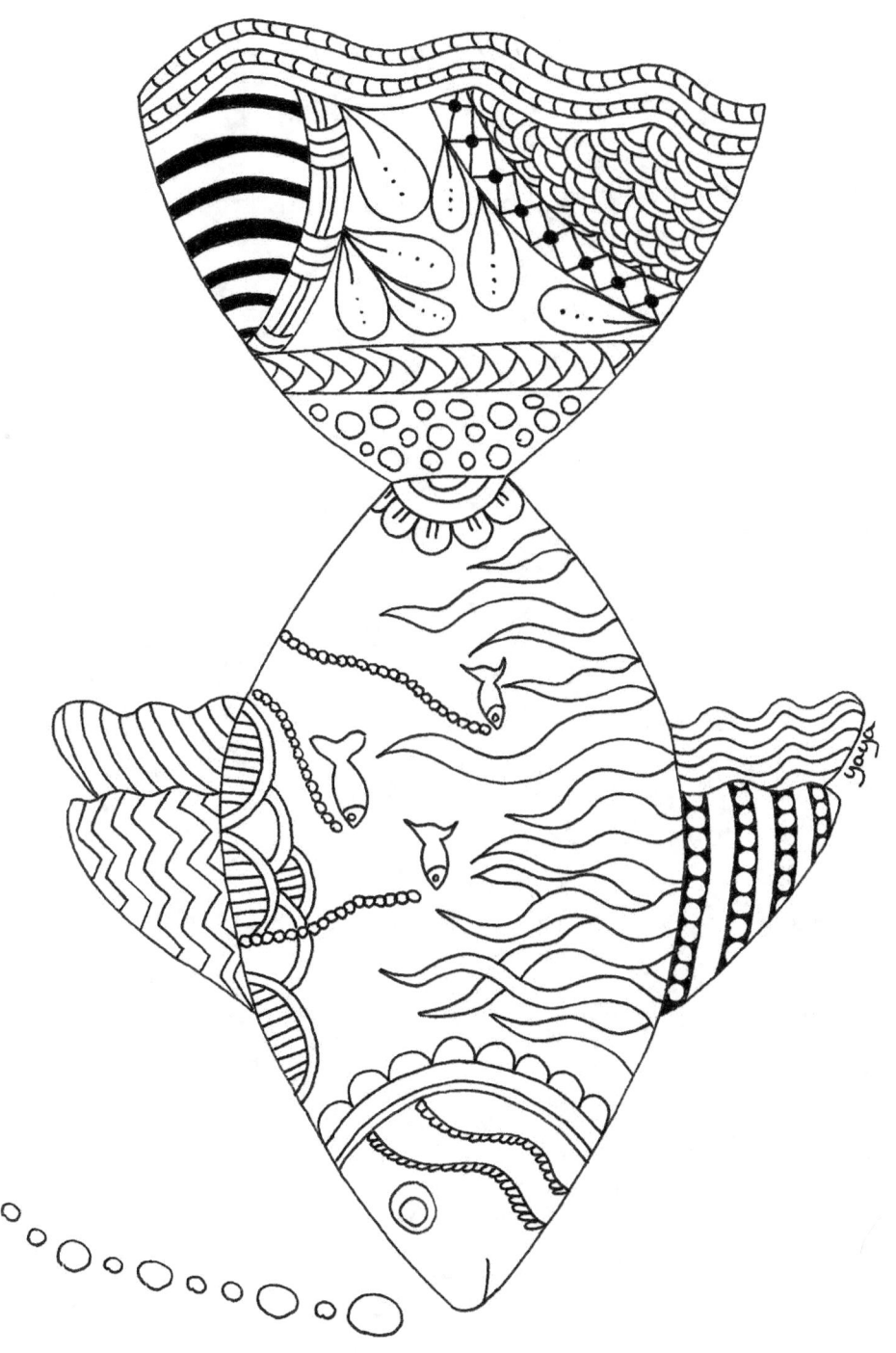

*Contributing Artist*
*Nancy Sutton Lewin*
*USA*

Facebook : iridescentbug

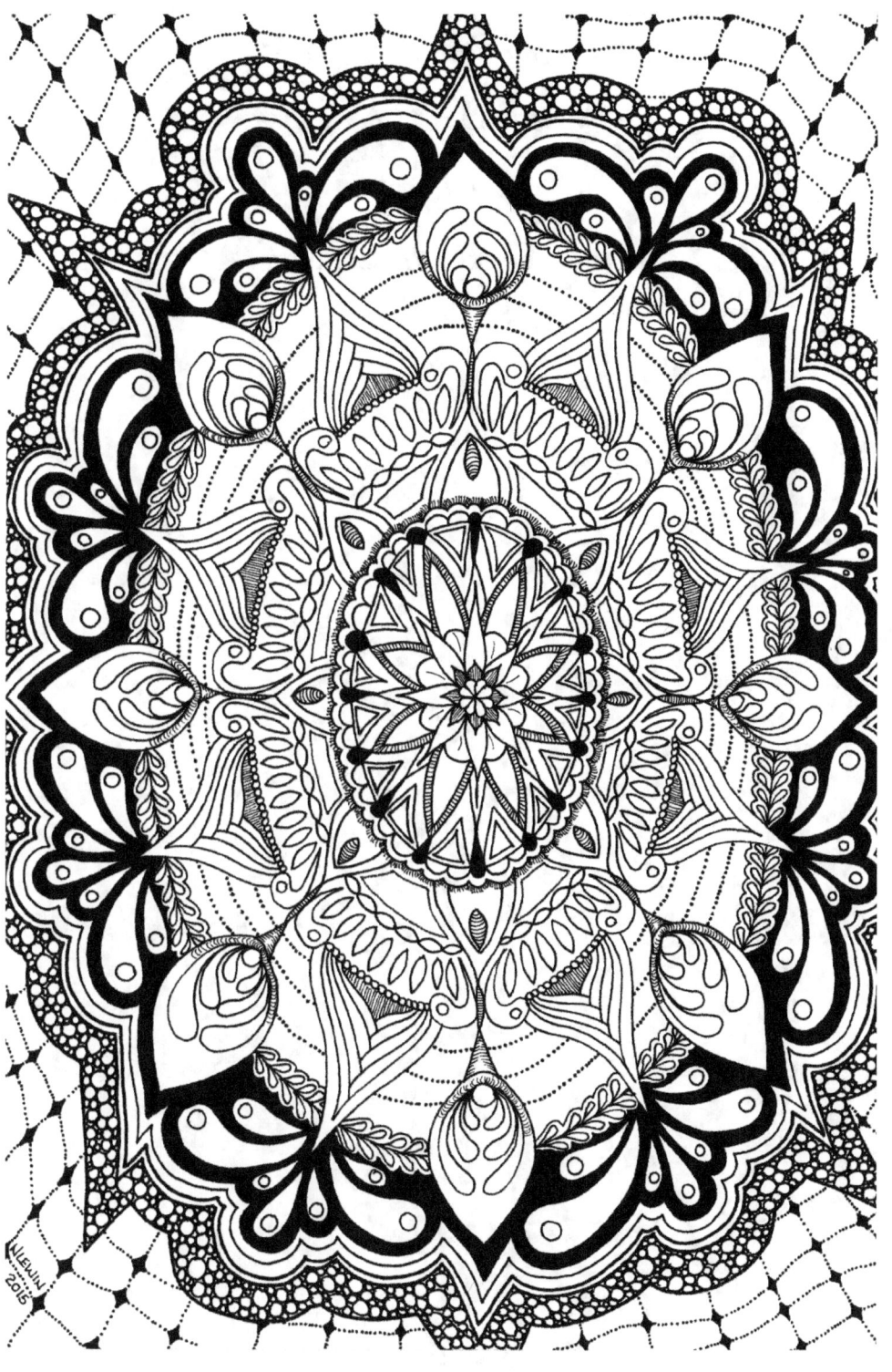

*Contributing Artist*
*Nancy Sutton Lewin*
*USA*

Facebook : iridescentbug

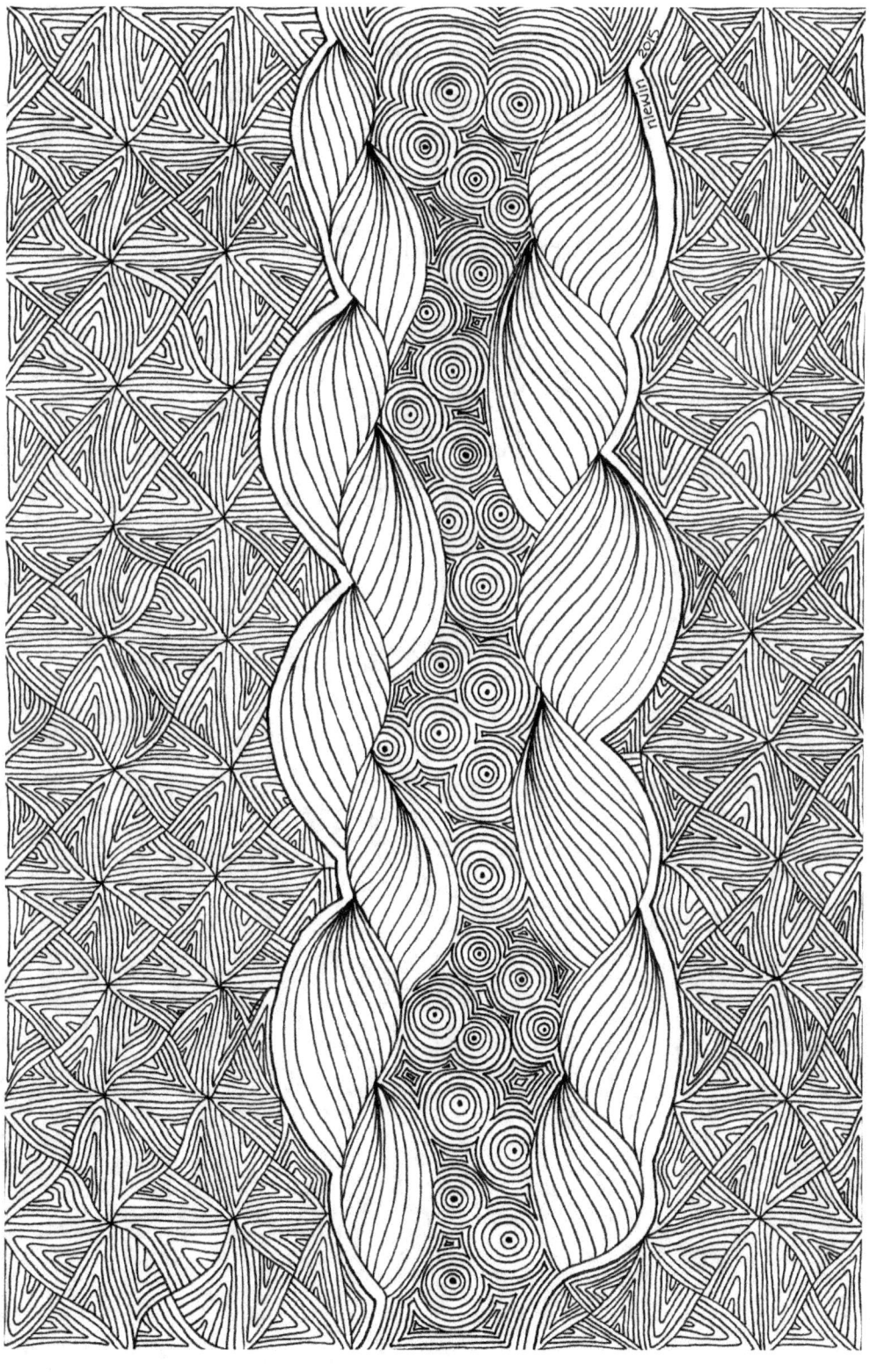

*Contributing Artist*
*Nancy Sutton Lewin*
*USA*

Facebook : iridescentbug

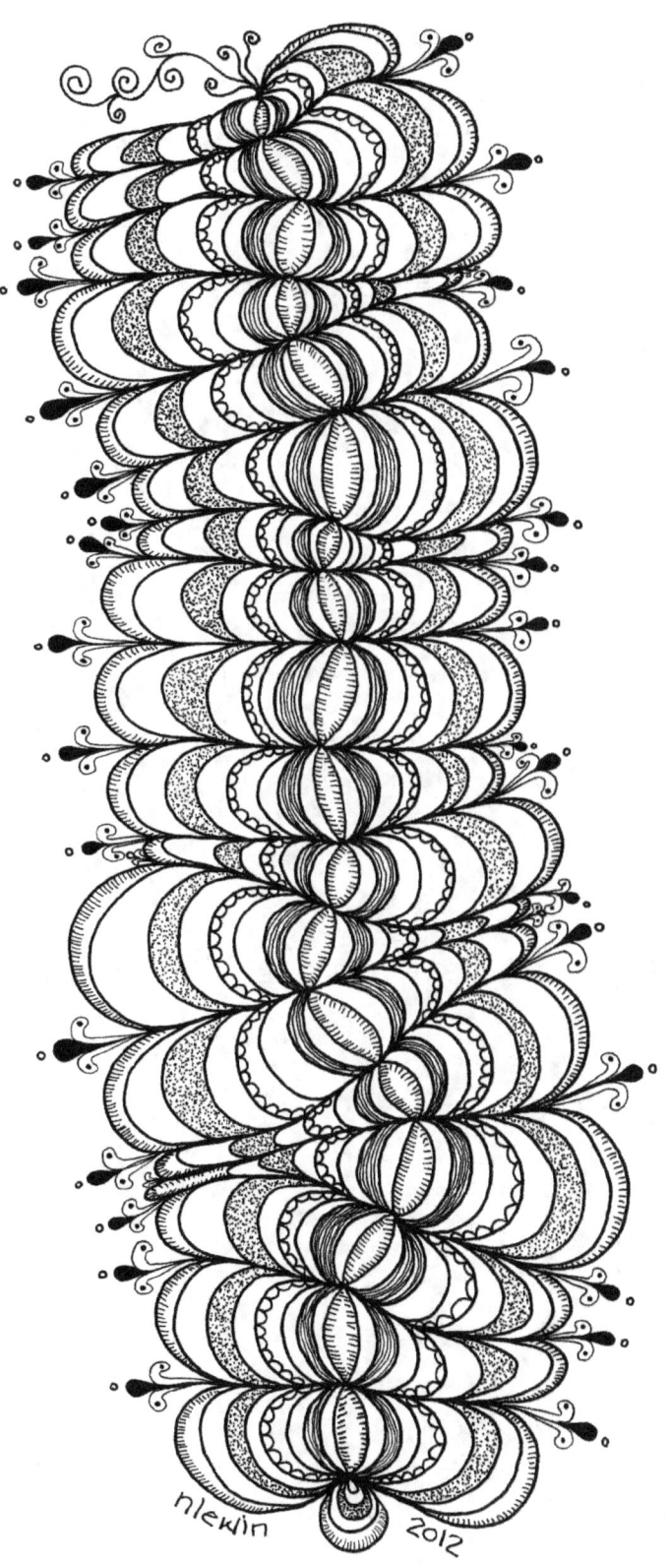

*Contributing Artist*
*Nancy Sutton Lewin*
*USA*

Facebook : iridescentbug

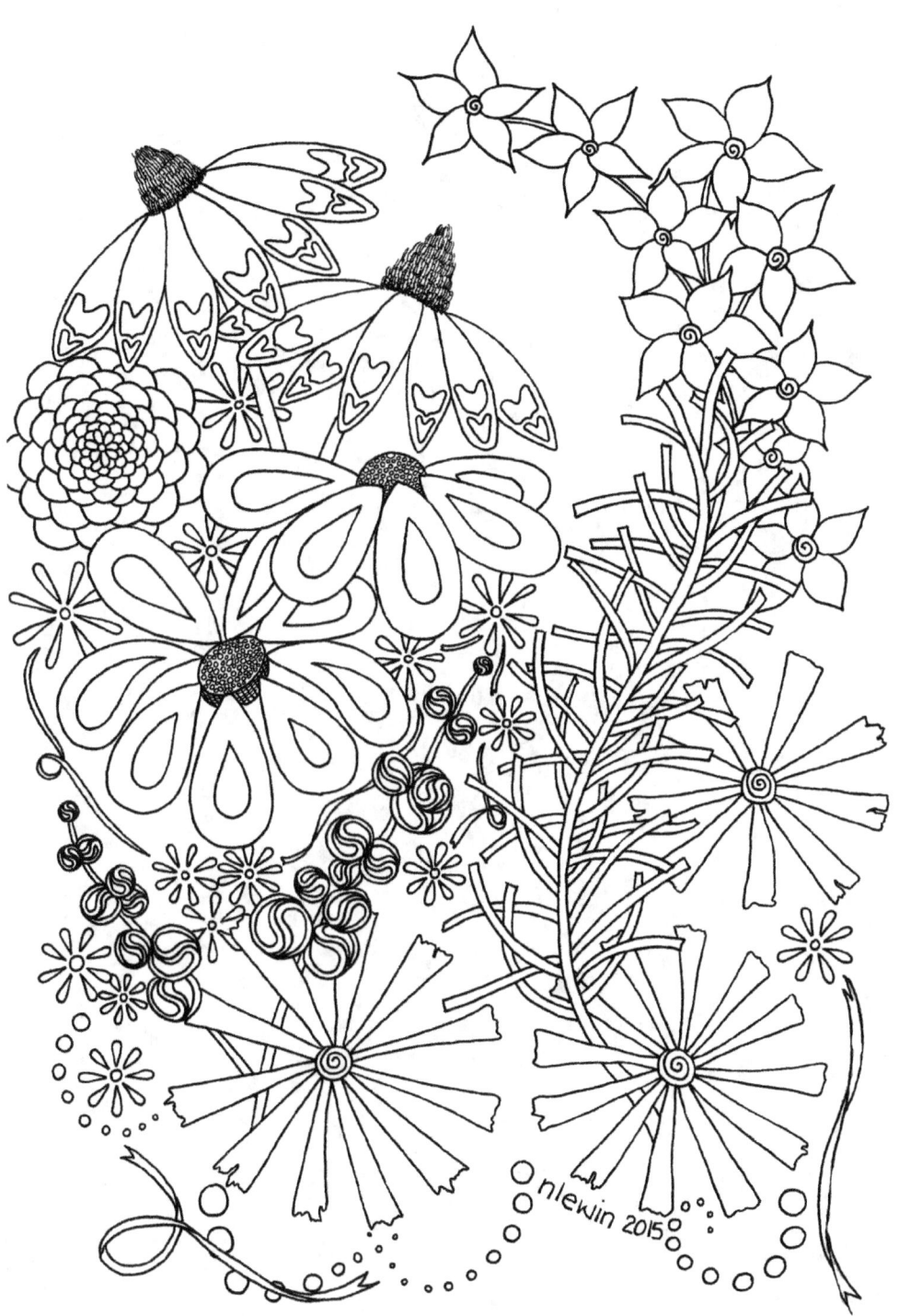

*Contributing Artist*
*Lynni Ex*
*UK*

Facebook : Lynni Ex

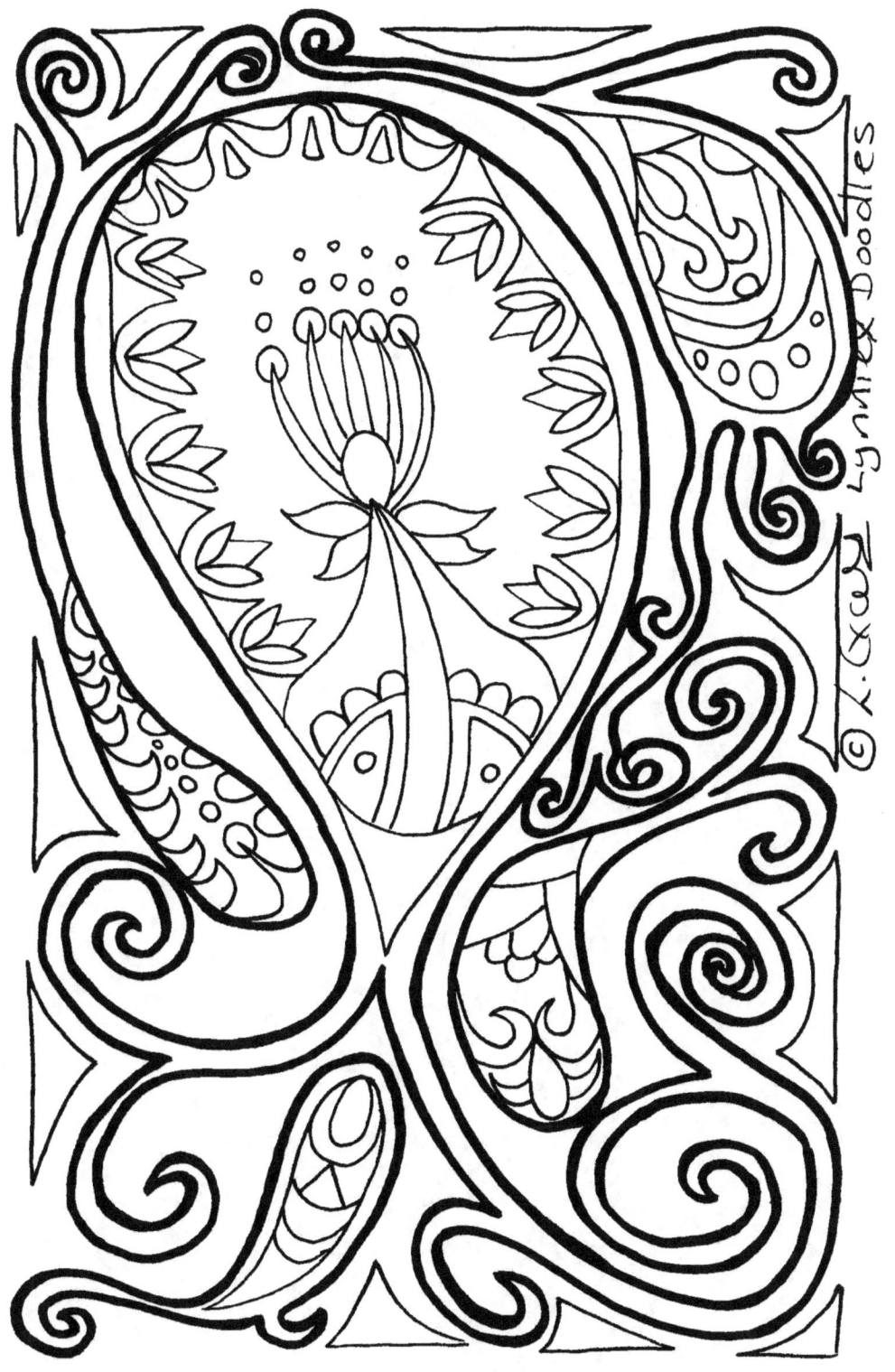

*Contributing Artist*
*Lynne McGee*
*Brisbane, Australia*

Facebook : Colorandtangle

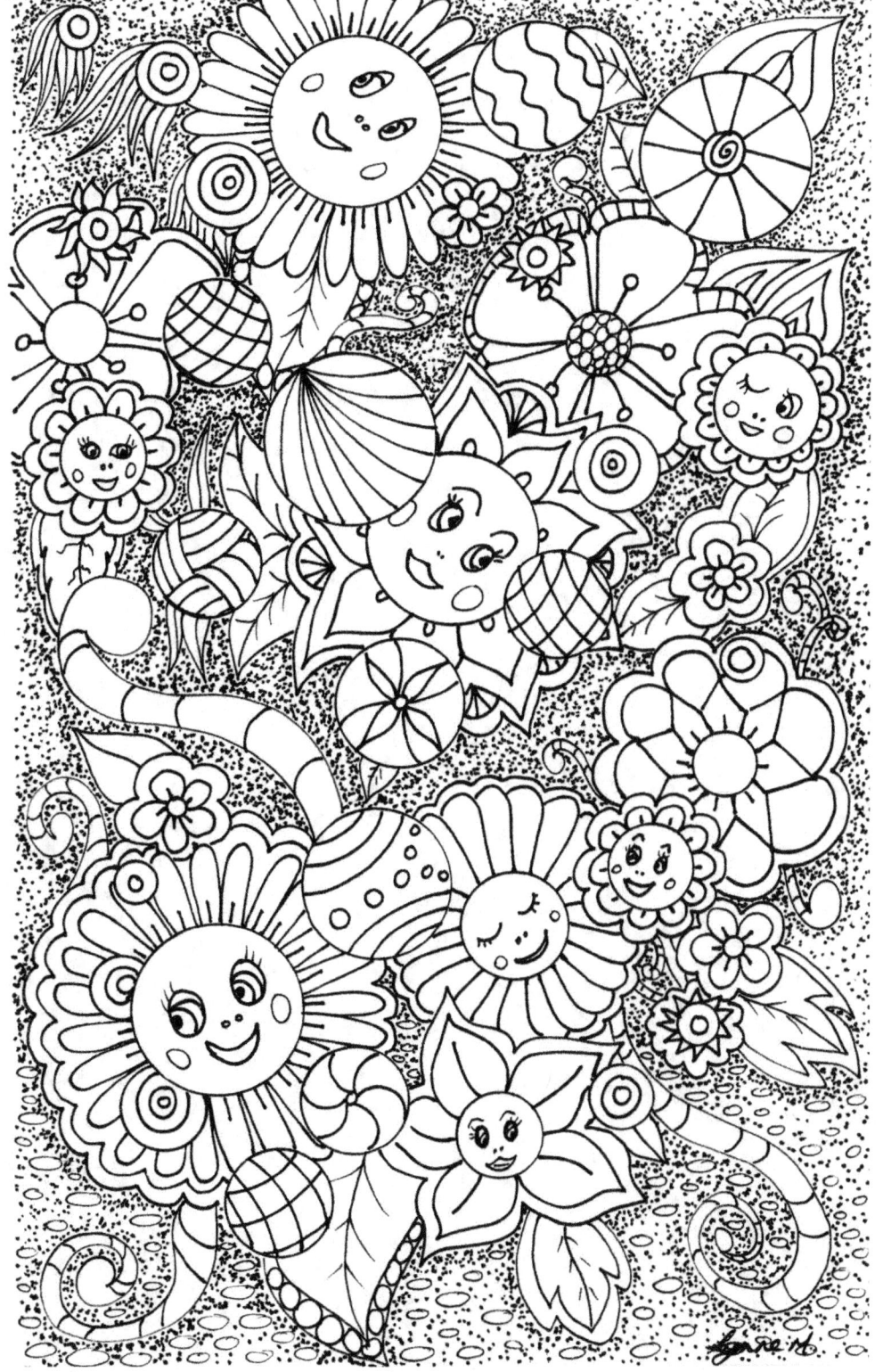

*Contributing Artist*
*Lynne McGee*
*Brisbane, Australia*

Facebook : Colorandtangle

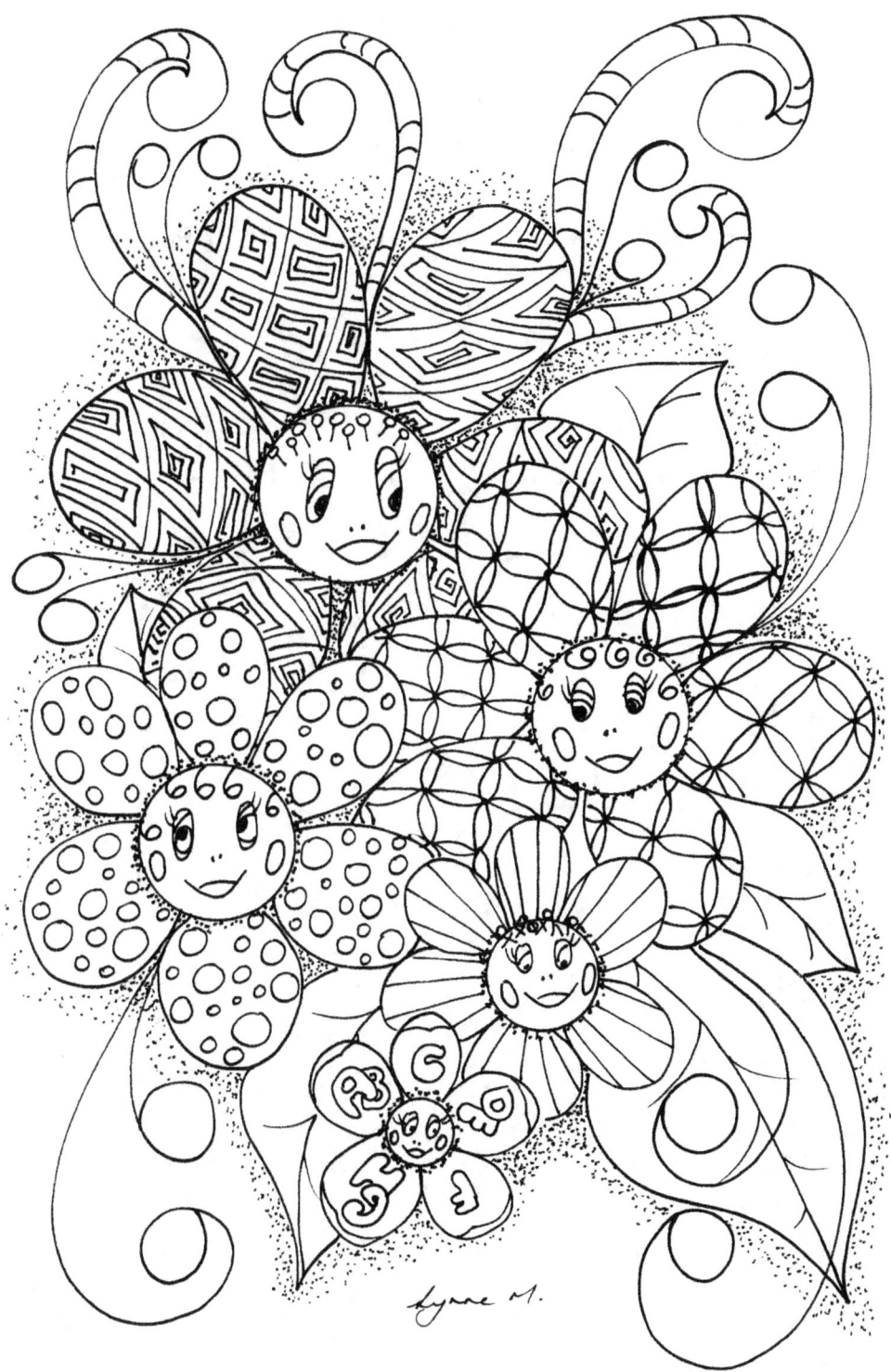

*Contributing Artist*
*Linda Karpinski*
*USA*

Facebook : Blue-Monkey-Kreations_Art-Page

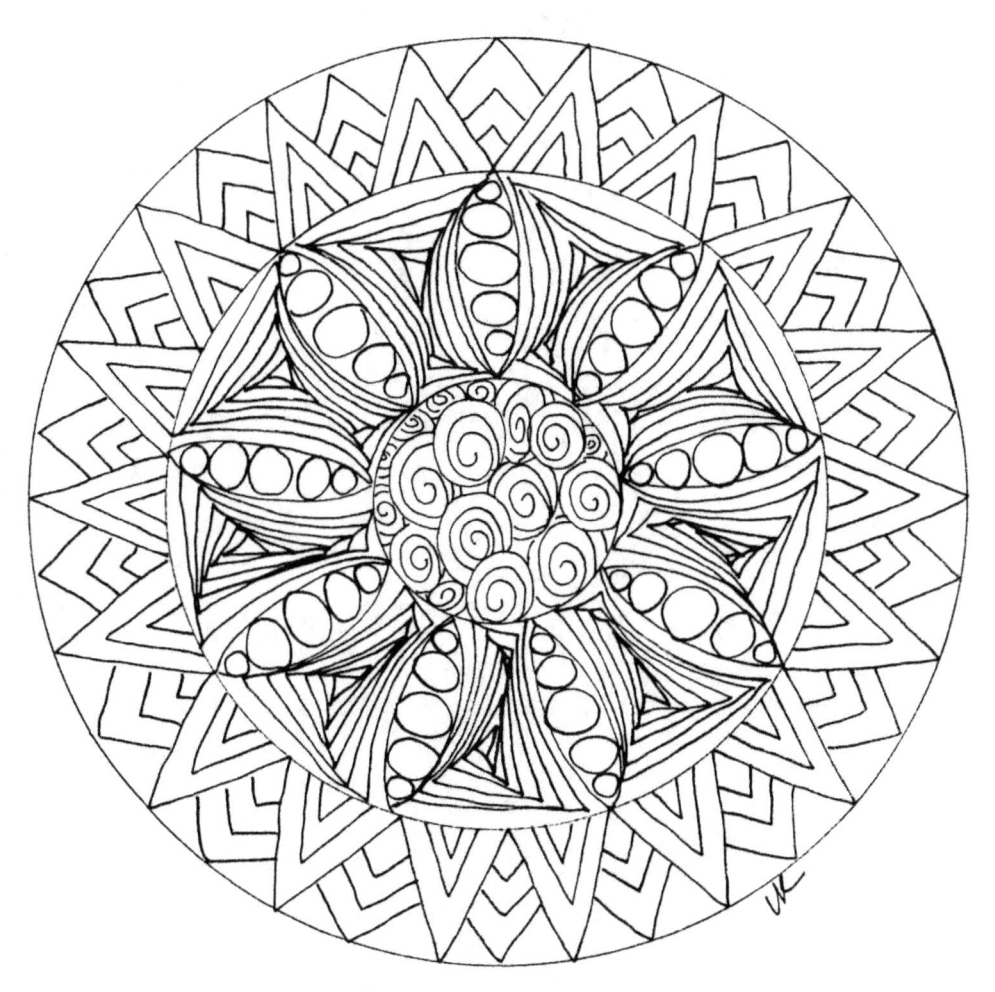

*Contributing Artist*
*Jane Levi*
*France*

Facebook: Cheeky Cats

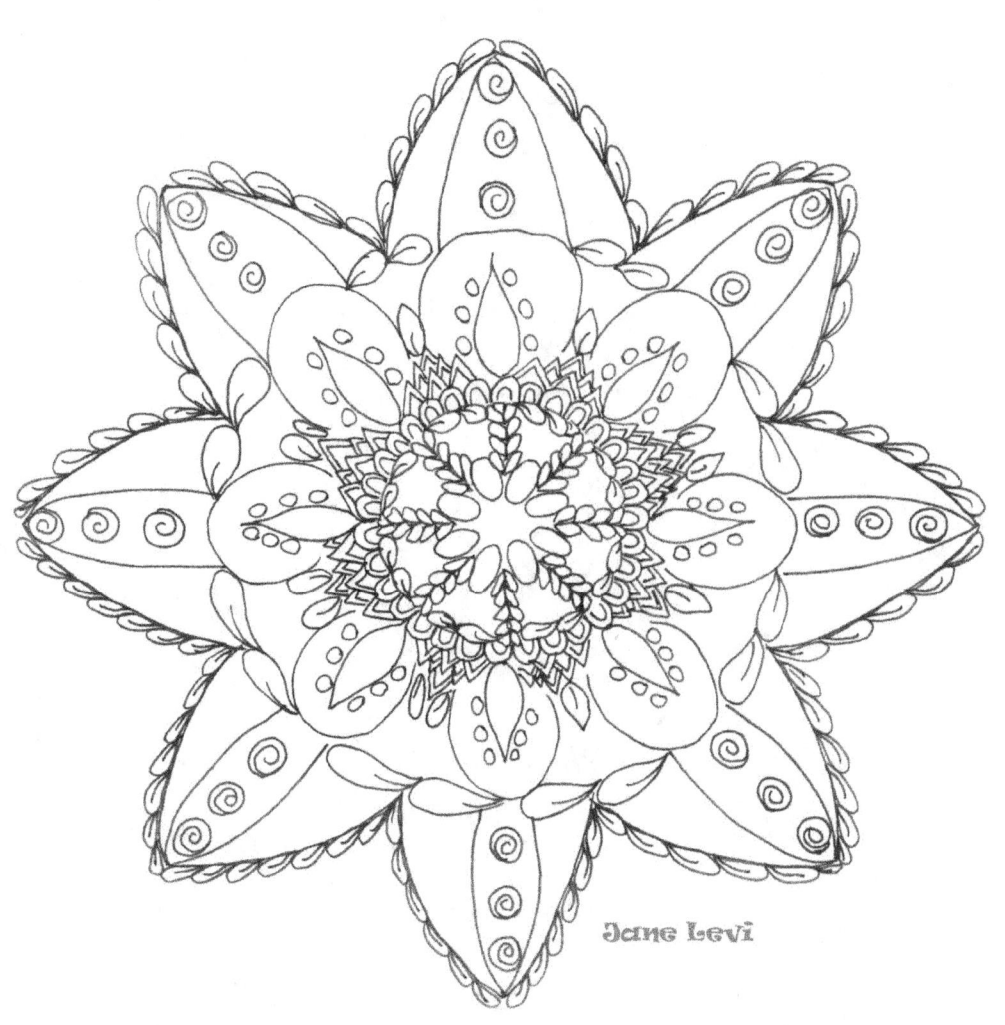

*Contributing Artist*
*Jane Levi*
*France*

Facebook: Cheeky Cats

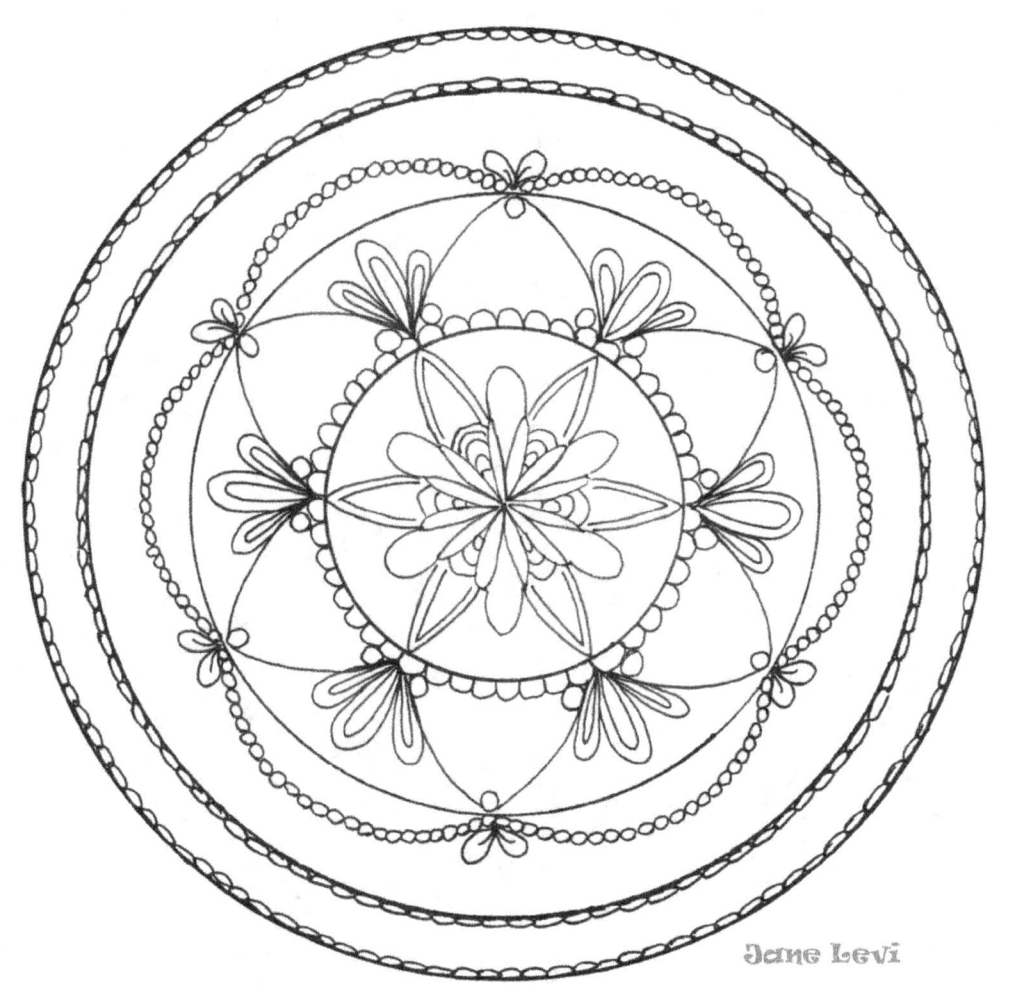

*Contributing Artist*
*Yaya*
*France*

Facebook : Les-gribouillis-de-yaya-georgia-merino

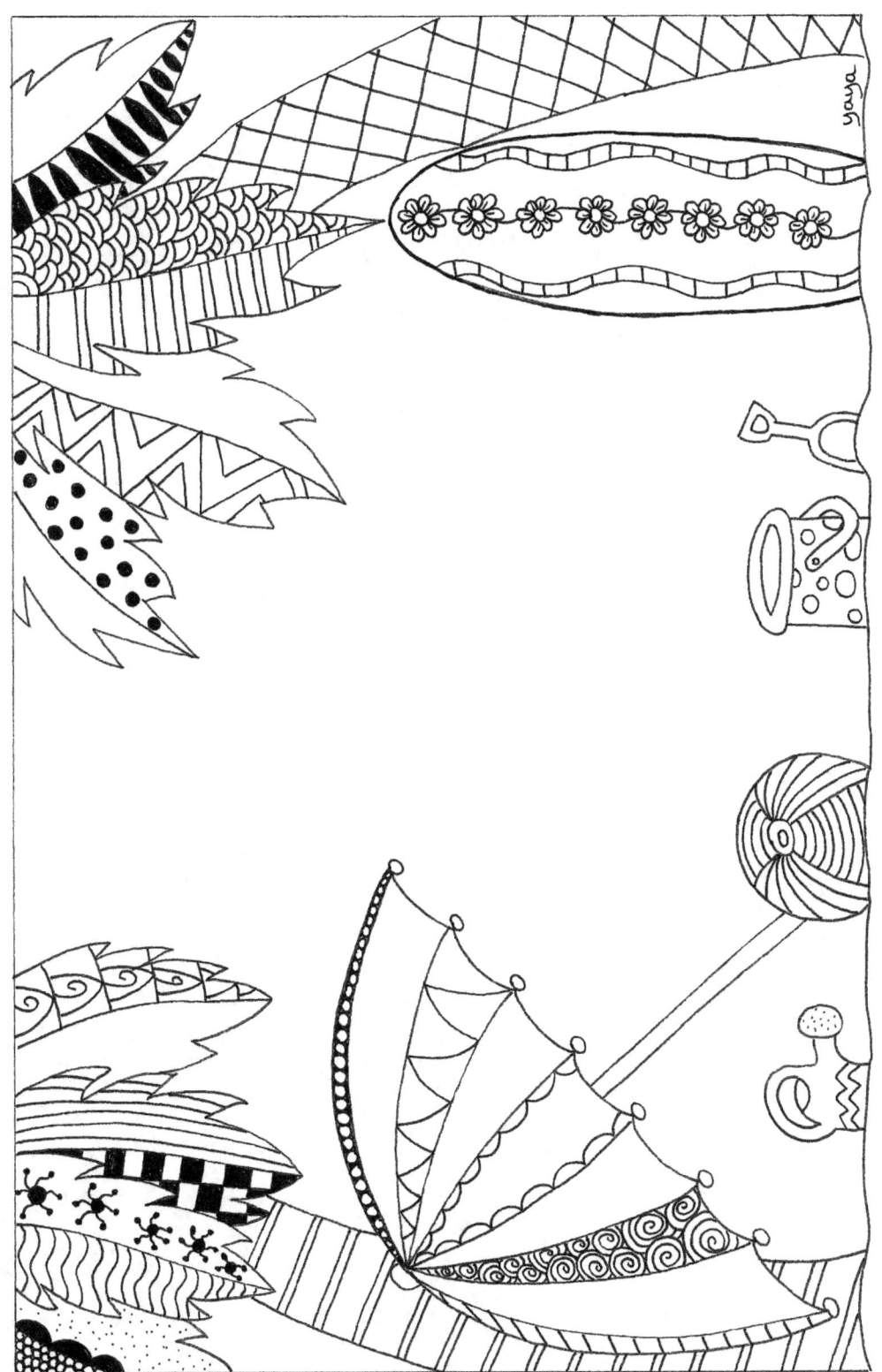

*Contributing Artist*
*Yaya*
*France*

Facebook : Les-gribouillis-de-yaya-georgia-merino

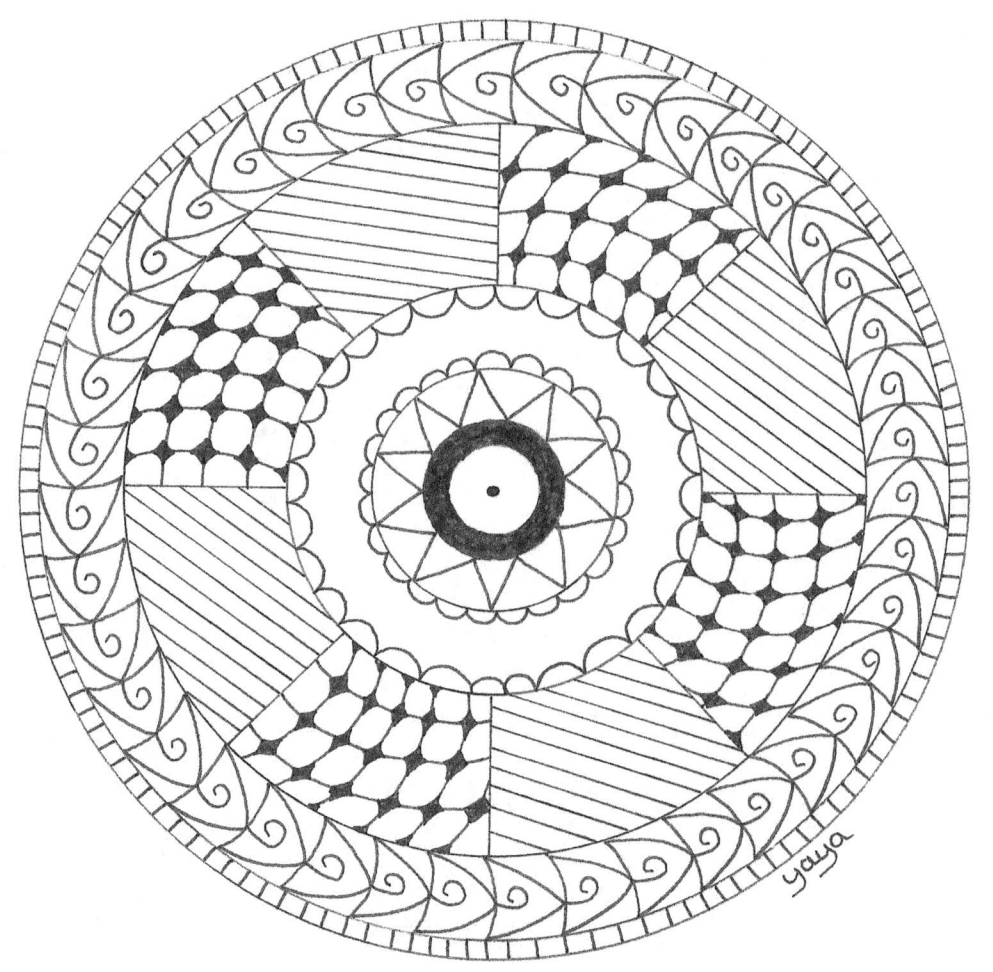

*Contributing Artist*
*DomDomx*
*France*

Facebook : Les-dessins-et-doodles-de-Dom-Domx

Facebook group : Color.Addict

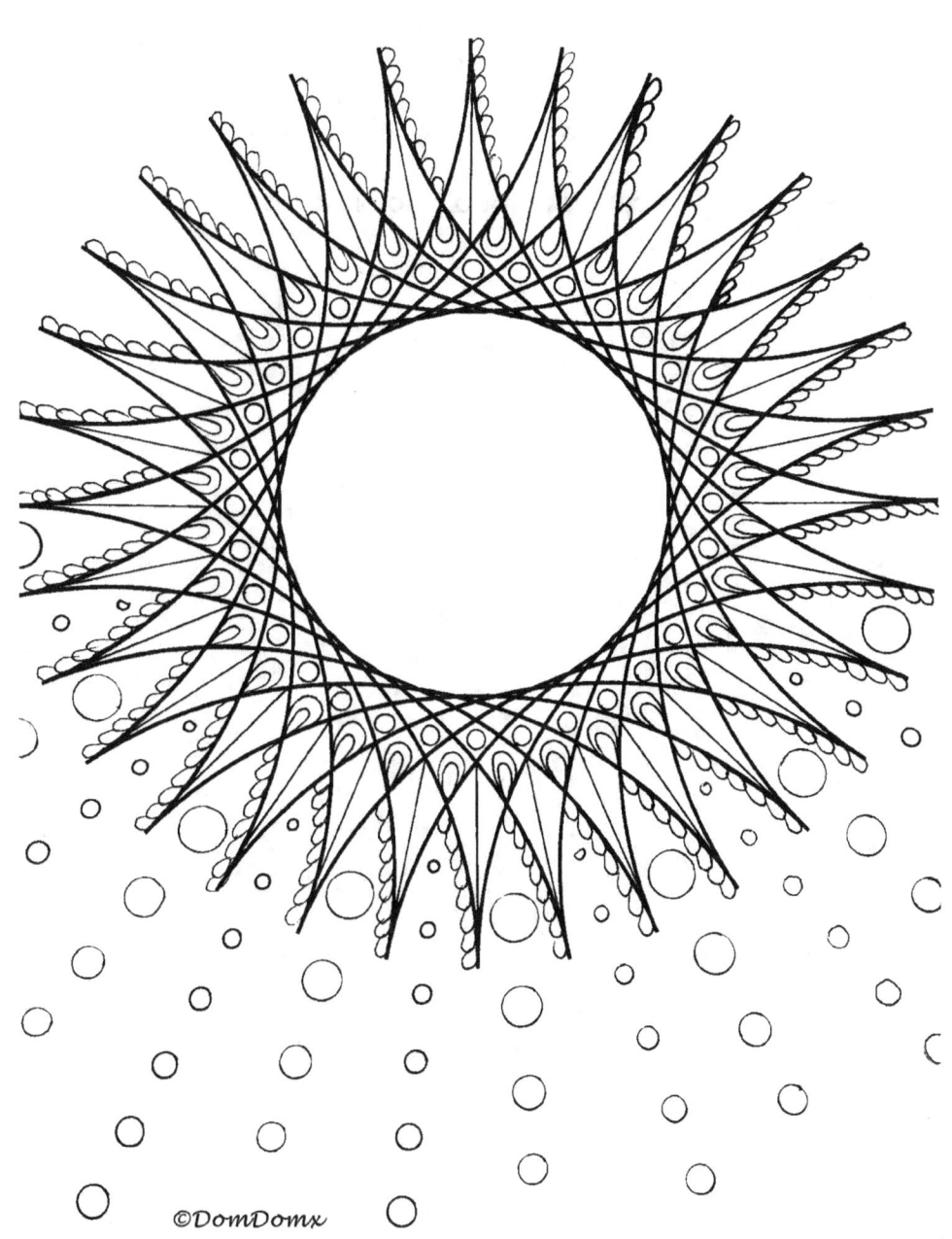

*Contributing Artist*
*DomDomx*
*France*

Facebook : Les-dessins-et-doodles-de-Dom-Domx

Facebook group : Color.Addict

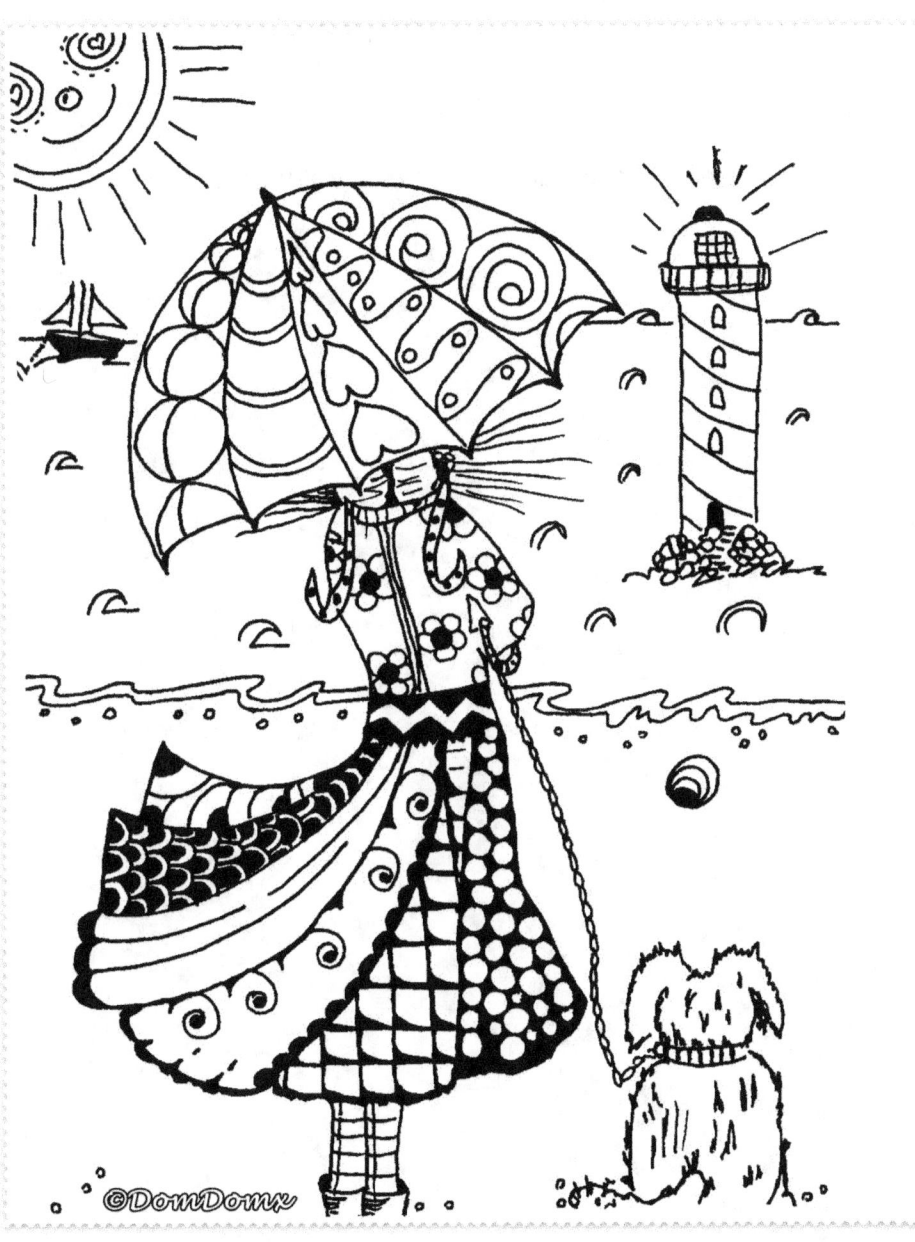

*Contributing Artist*
*Dianne Comeau*
*Canada*

Web : diannecomeau.wordpress.com

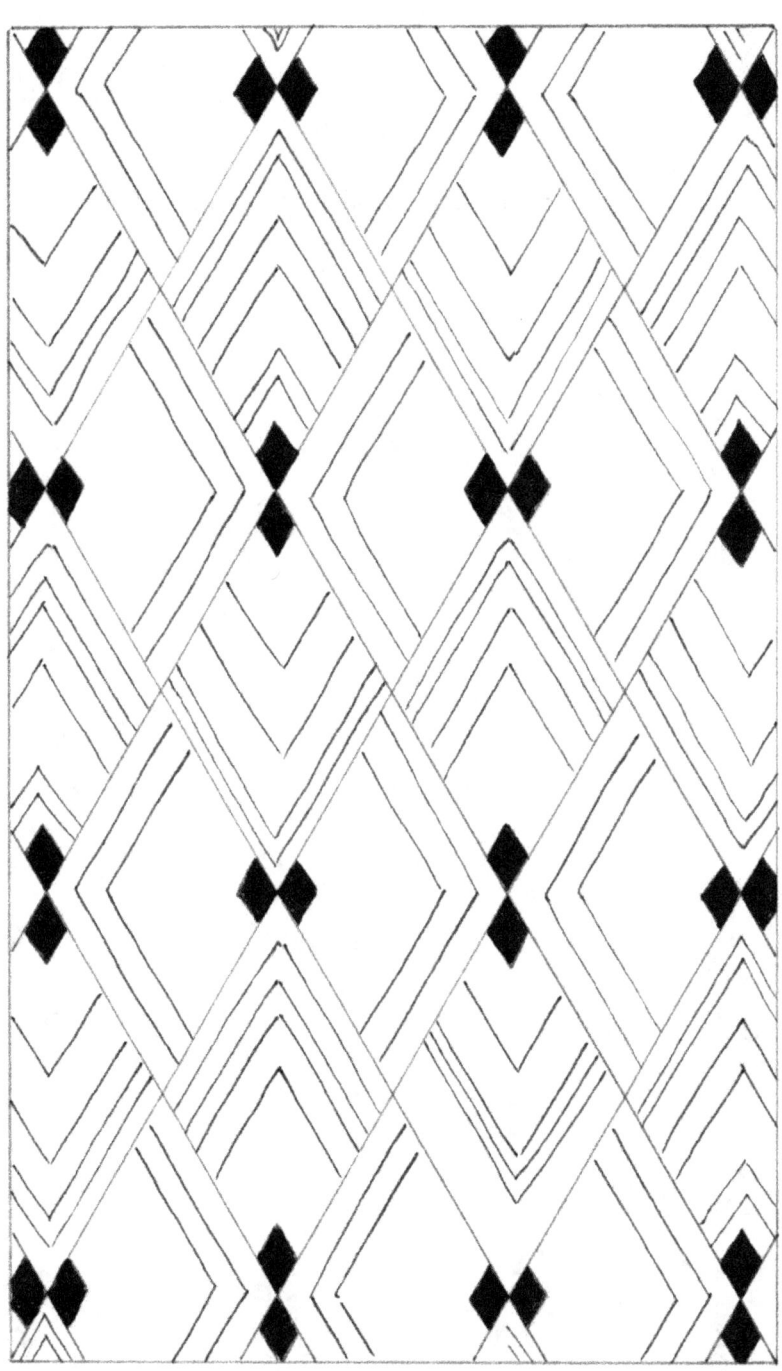

*Contributing Artist*
*Dianne Comeau*
*Canada*

Web : diannecomeau.wordpress.com

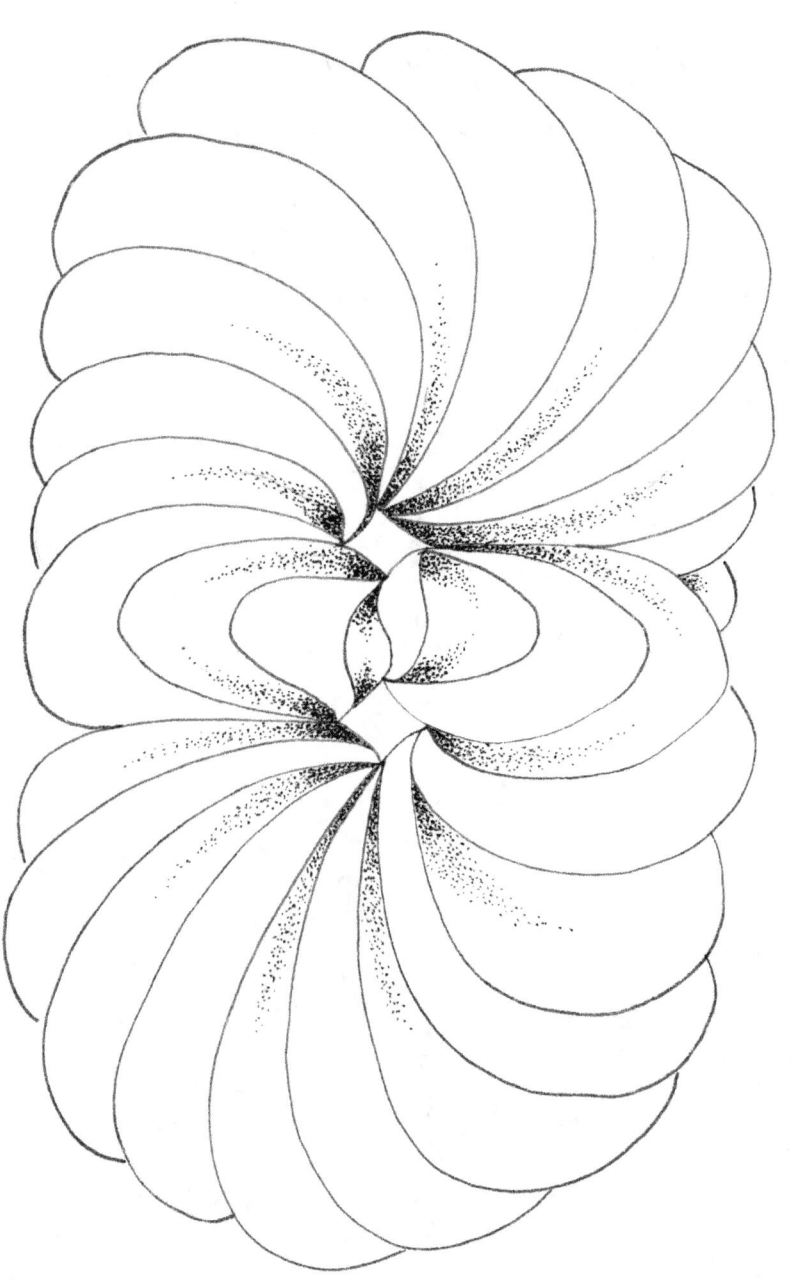

*Contributing Artist*
*Dianne Comeau*
*Canada*

Web : diannecomeau.wordpress.com

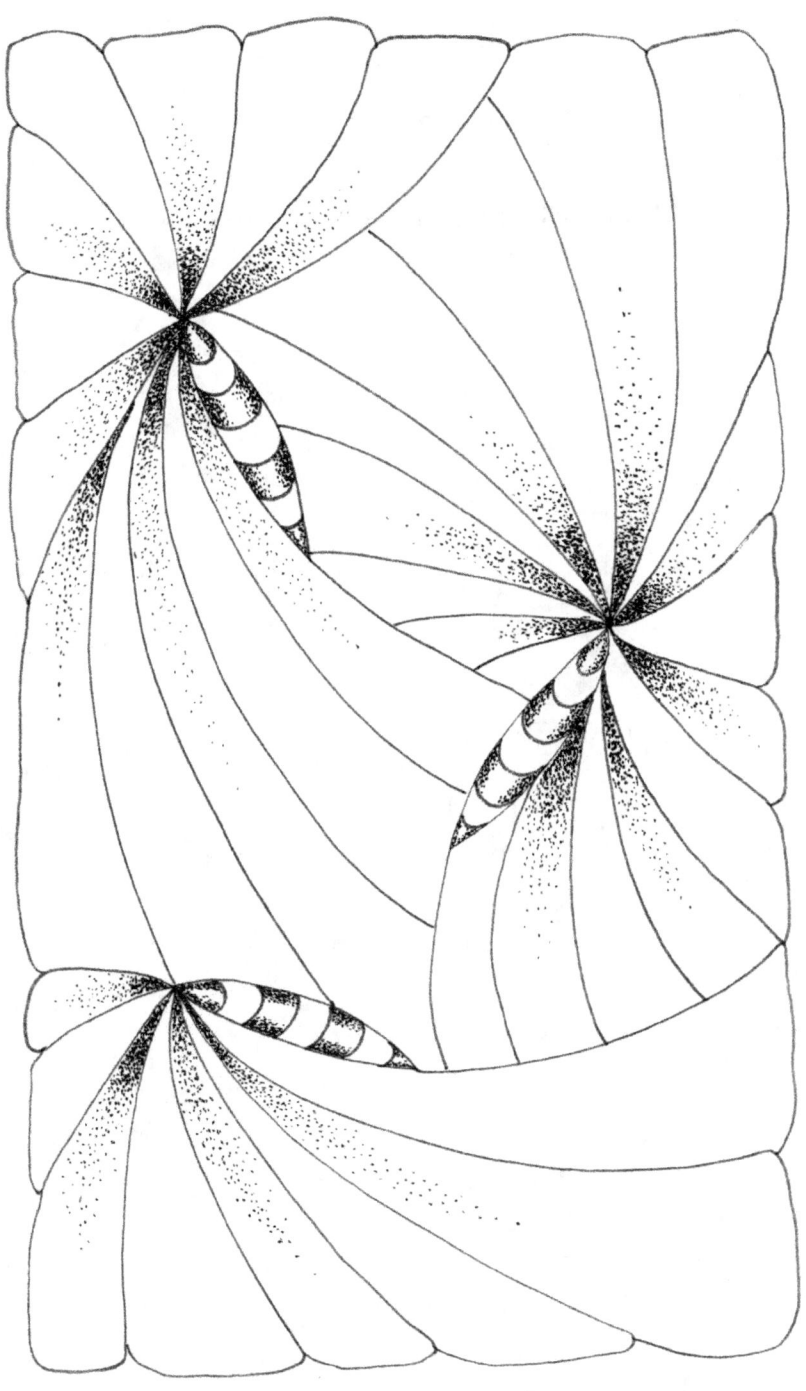

*Contributing Artist*
*Dianne Comeau*
*Canada*

Web : diannecomeau.wordpress.com

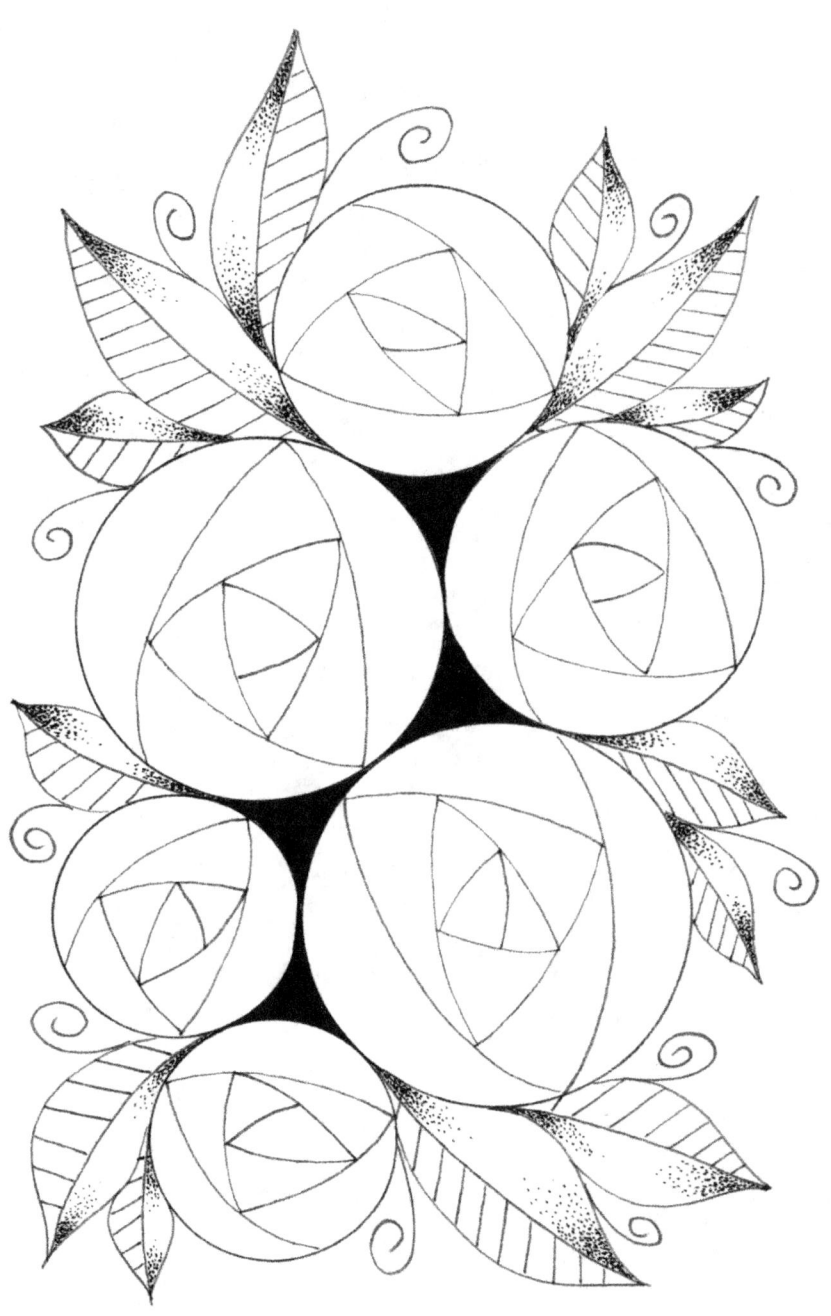

*Contributing Artist*
*Johanna Ans*
*The Netherlands*

Web : claukemp72.wordpress.com

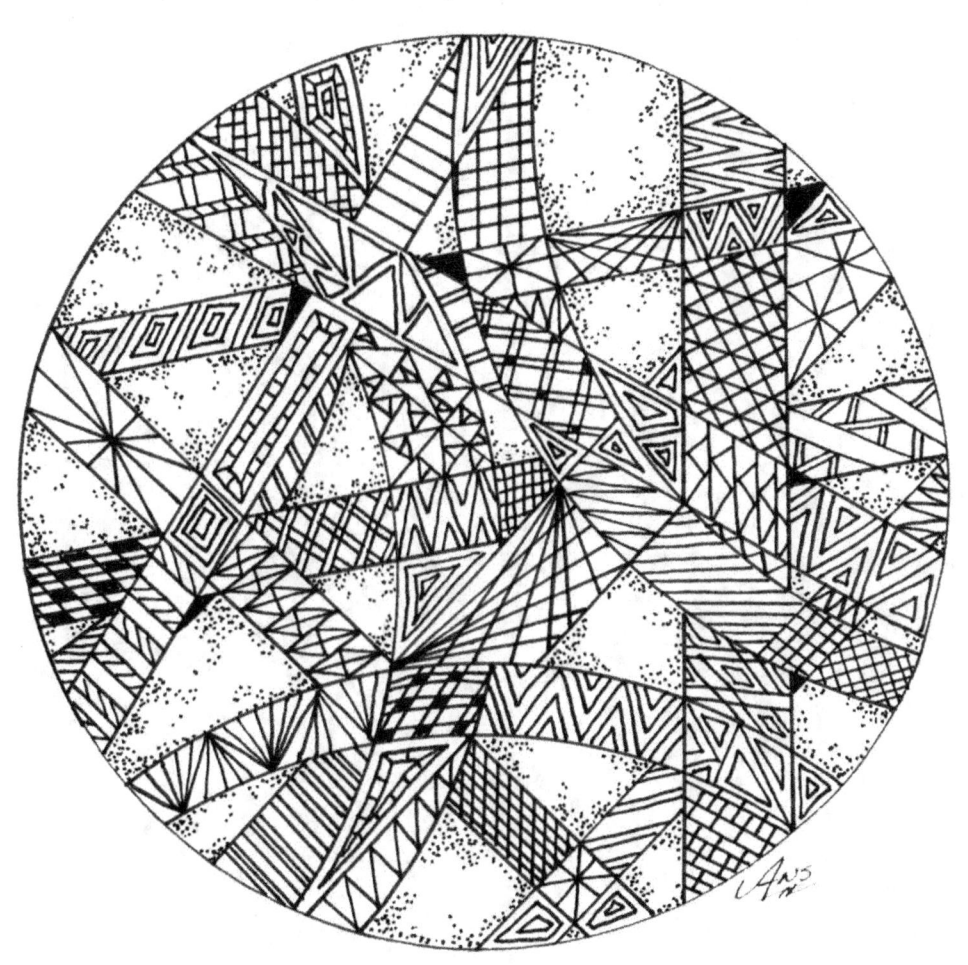

*Contributing Artist*
*Linda Karpinski*
*USA*

Facebook : Blue-Monkey-Kreations_Art-Page

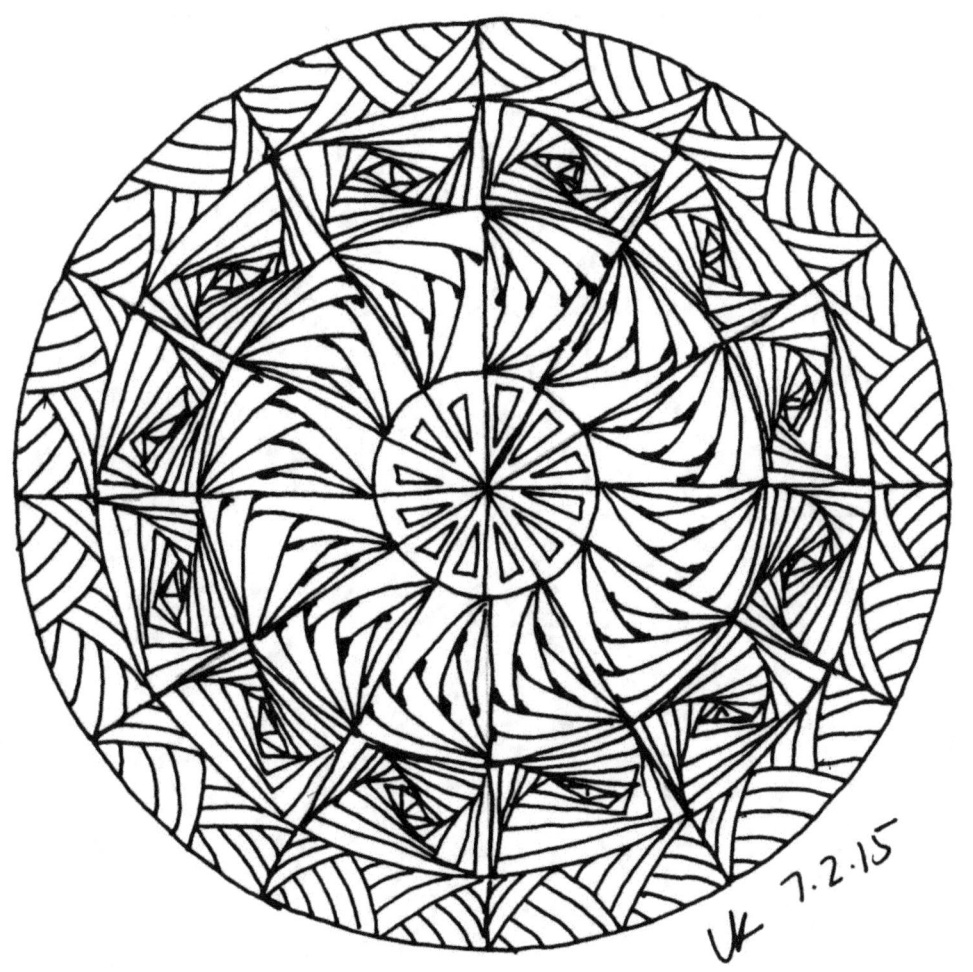

*Contributing Artist*
*Linda Karpinski*
*USA*

Facebook : Blue-Monkey-Kreations_Art-Page

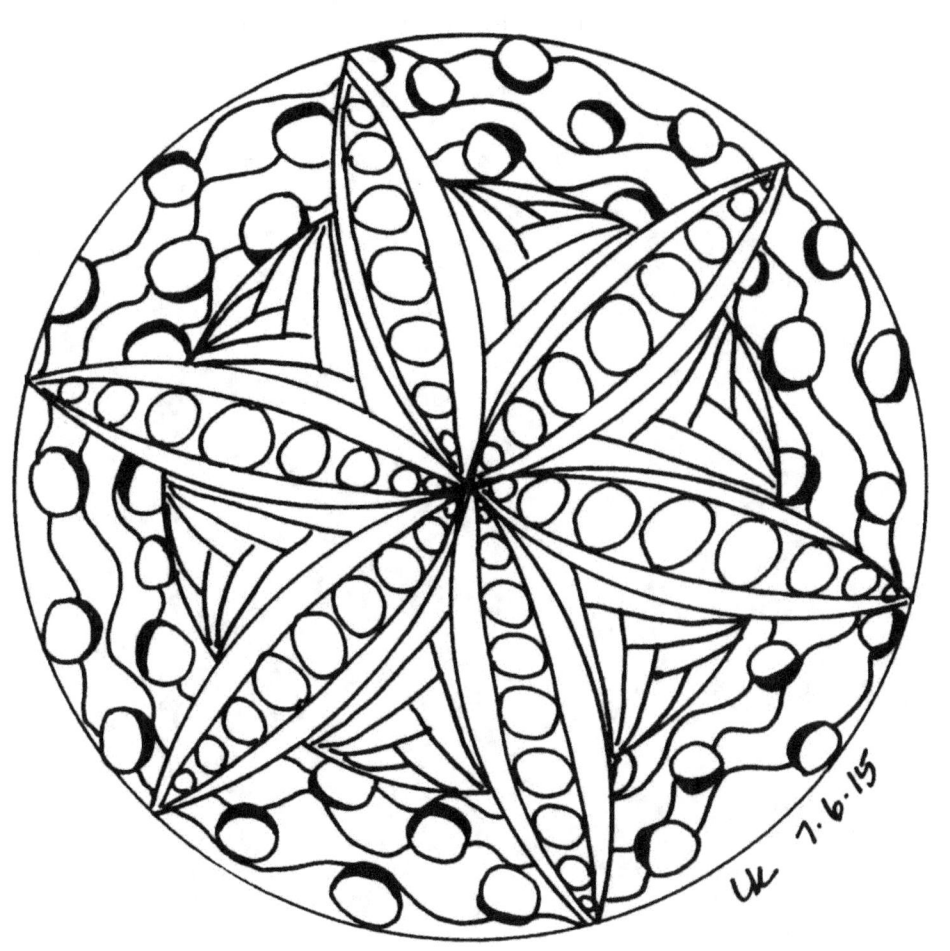

*Contributing Artist*
*Linda Karpinski*
*USA*

Facebook : Blue-Monkey-Kreations_Art-Page

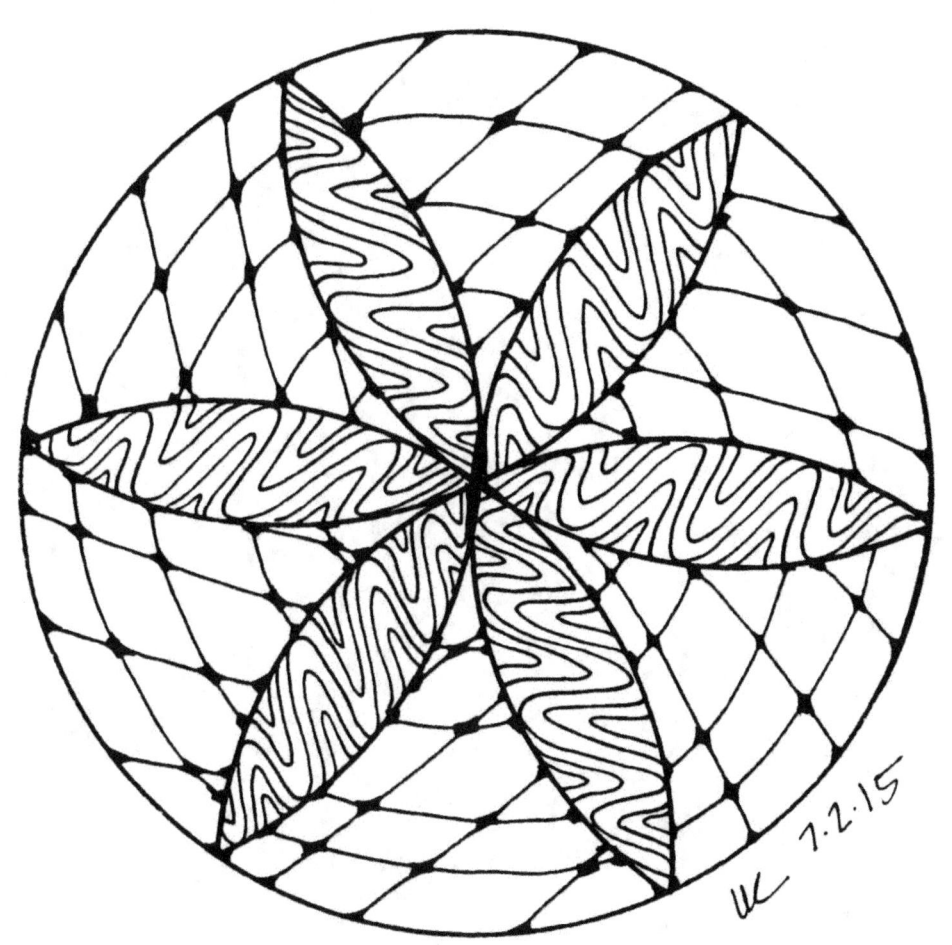

*Contributing Artist*
*Iben Lykke Højholdt*
*Denmark*

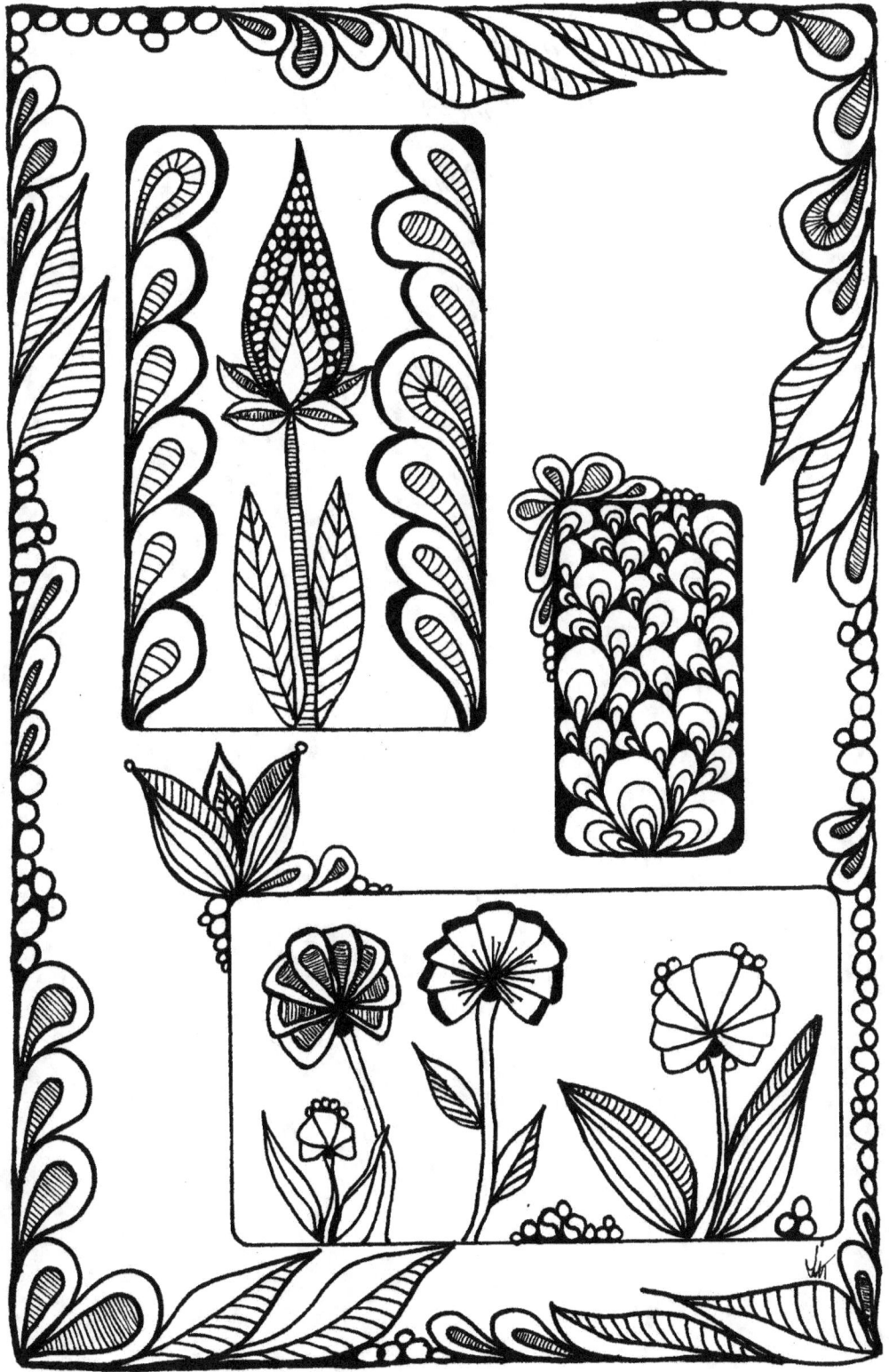

*Contributing Artist
Iben Lykke Højholdt
Denmark*

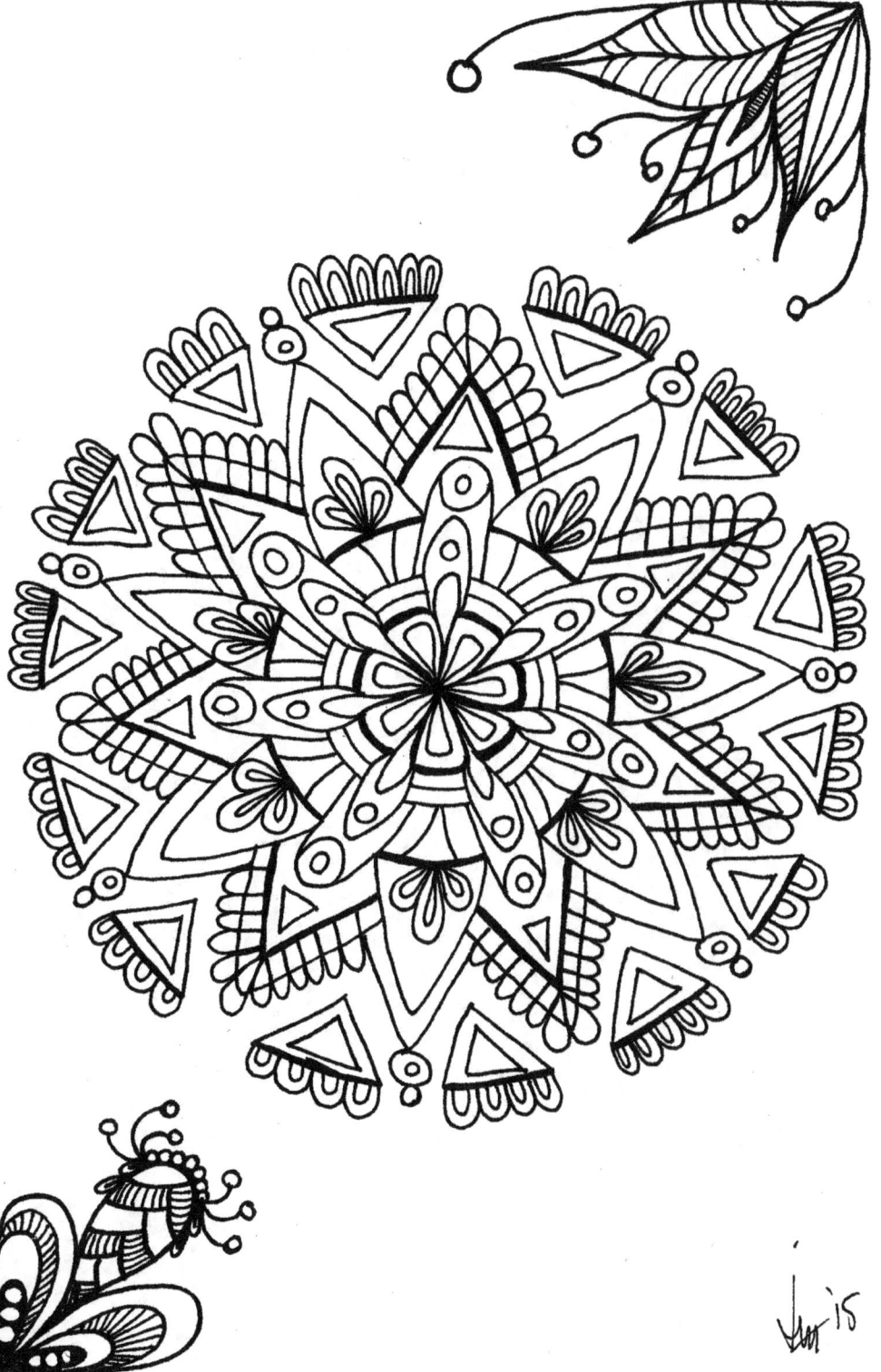

*Contributing Artist*
*Iben Lykke Højholdt*
*Denmark*

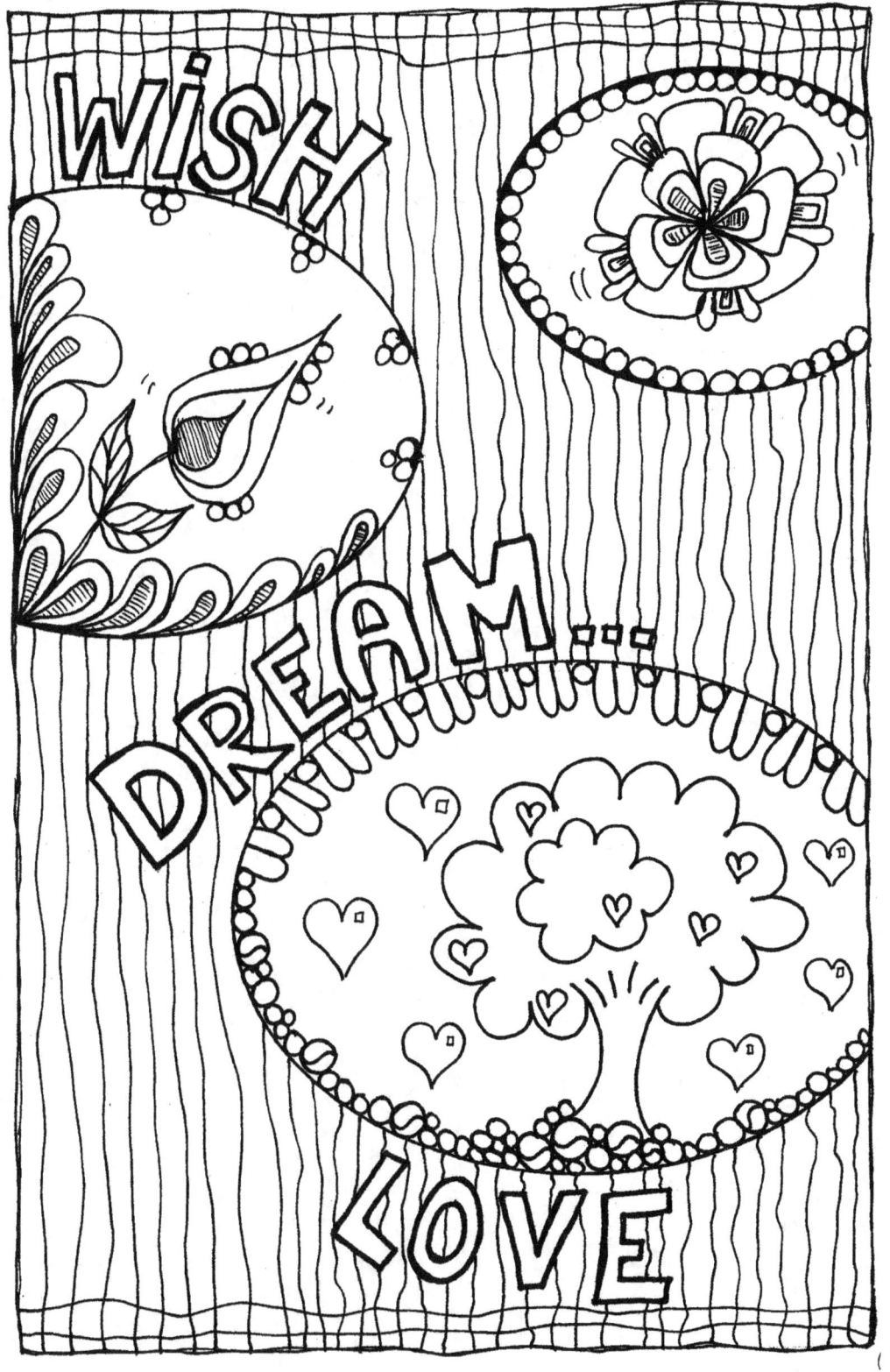

*Contributing Artist*
*Bev Choy*
*USA*

Facebook : bevchoyart

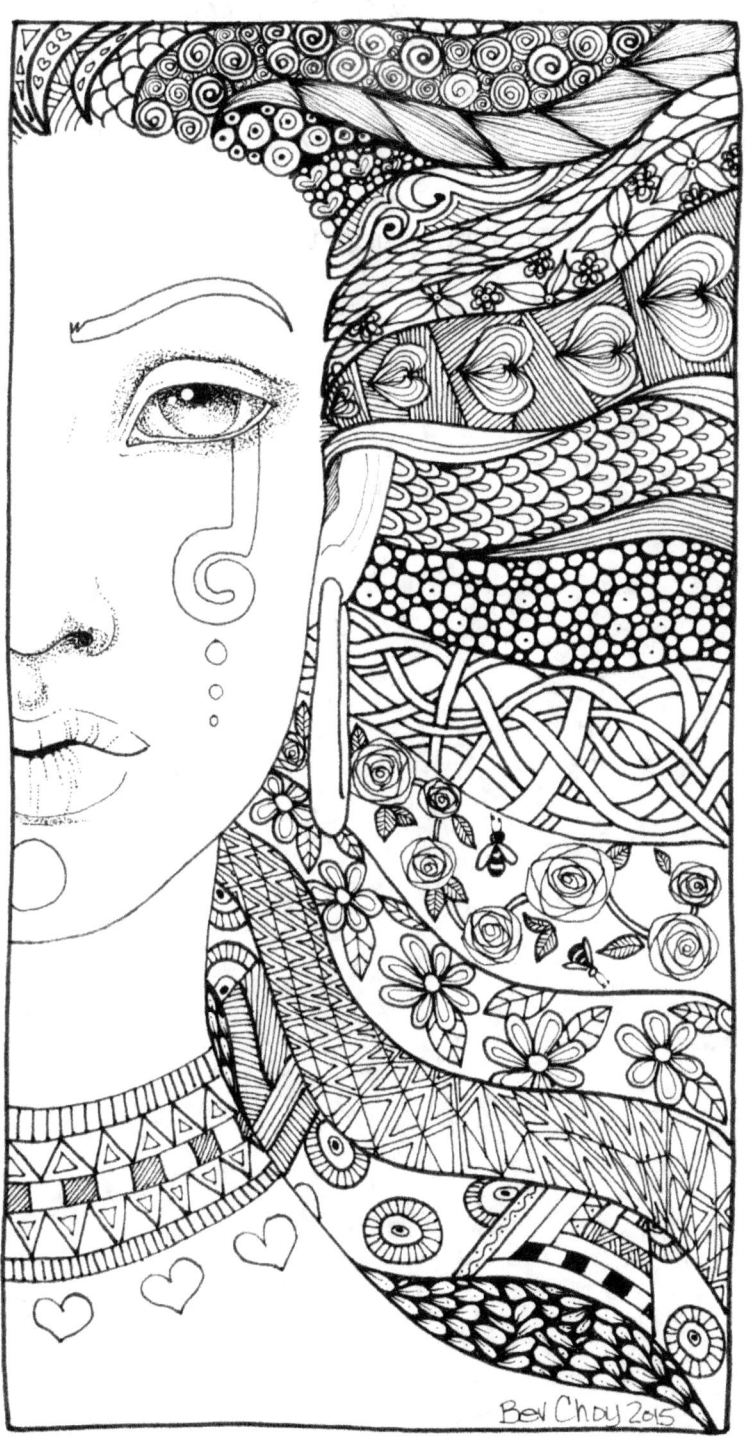

*Contributing Artist*
*Velvet Comeau*
*Canada*

Facebook : tranquilmoonart

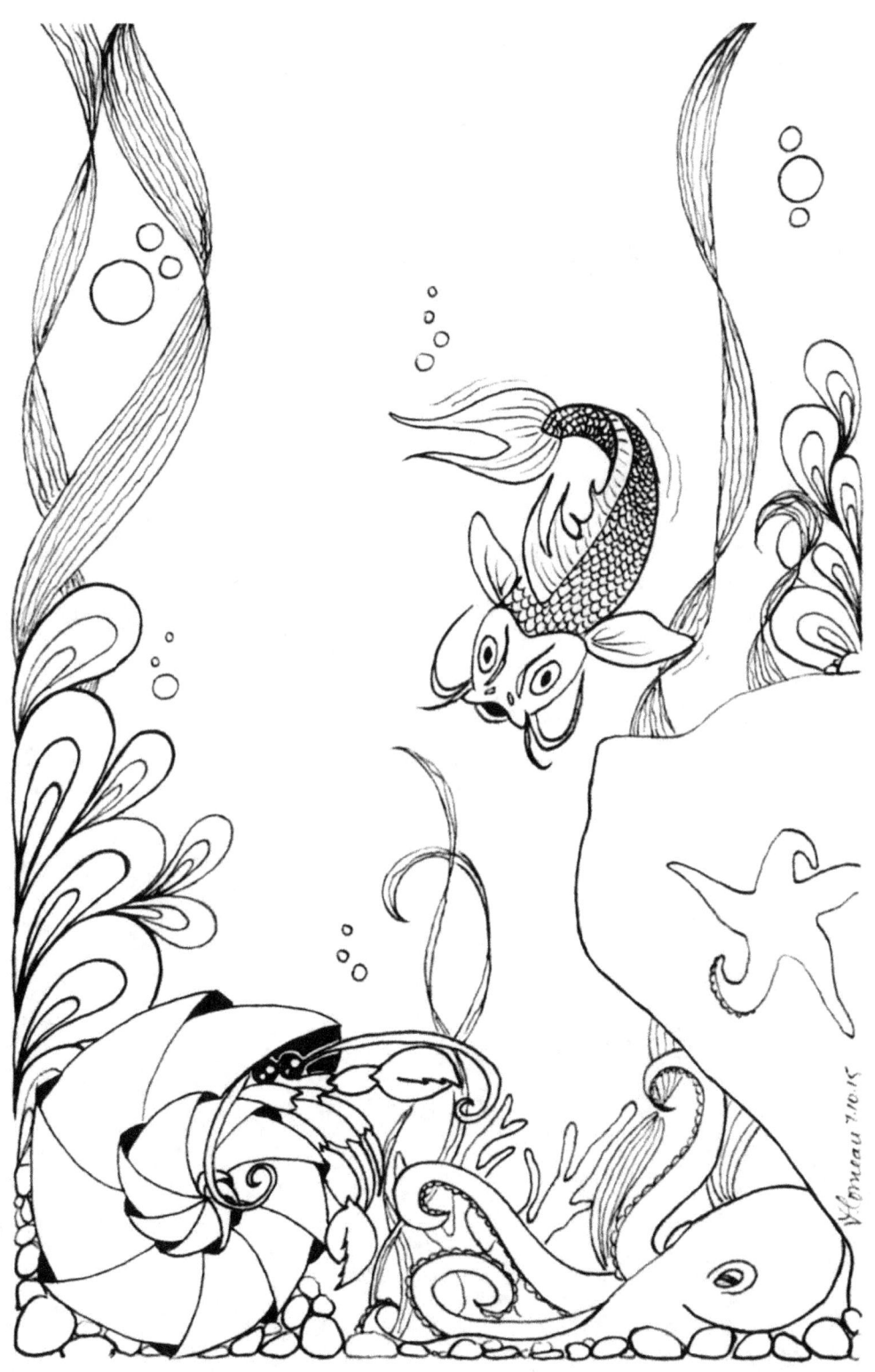

*Contributing Artist*
*Johanna Ans*
*The Netherlands*

Web : claukemp72.wordpress.com

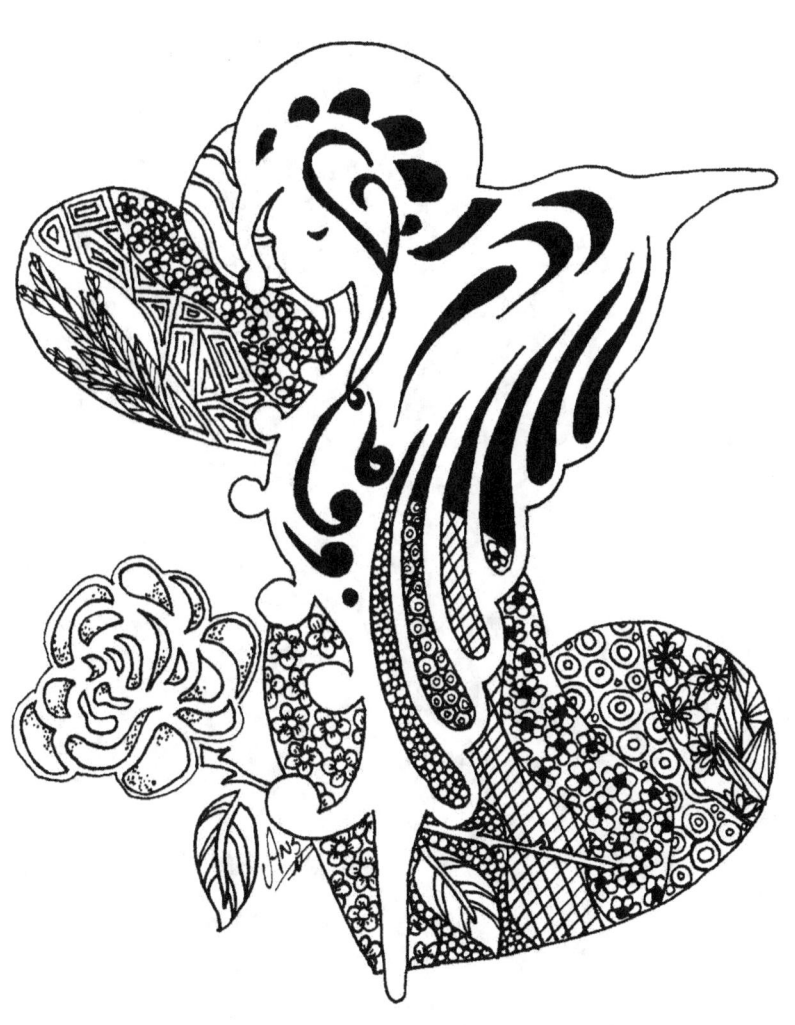

*Contributing Artist*
*Johanna Ans*
*The Netherlands*

Web : claukemp72.wordpress.com

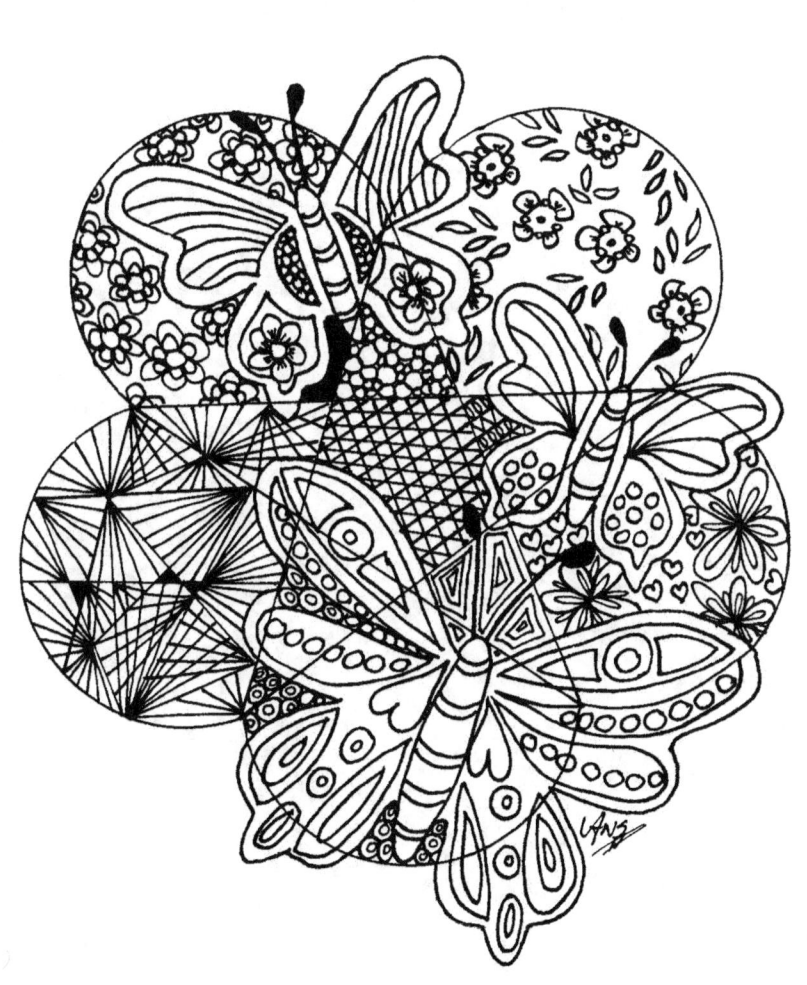

*Contributing Artist*
*Johanna Ans*
*The Netherlands*

Web : claukemp72.wordpress.com

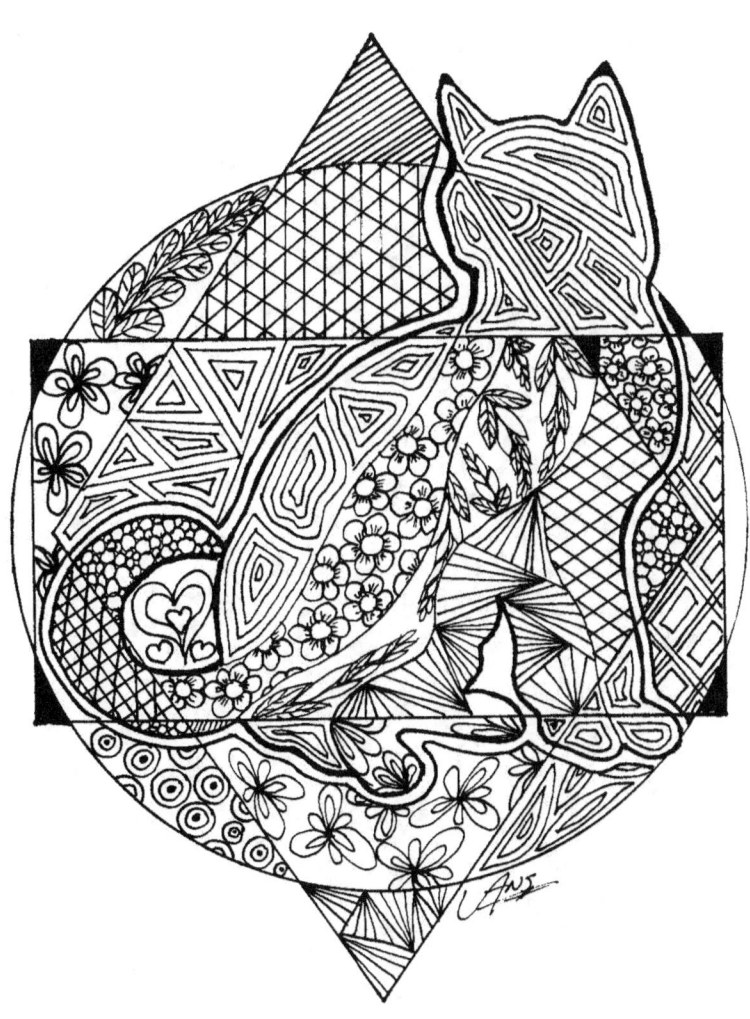

*Contributing Artist*
*Tammy Stansbery*
*USA*

Facebook : TJsArtCorner

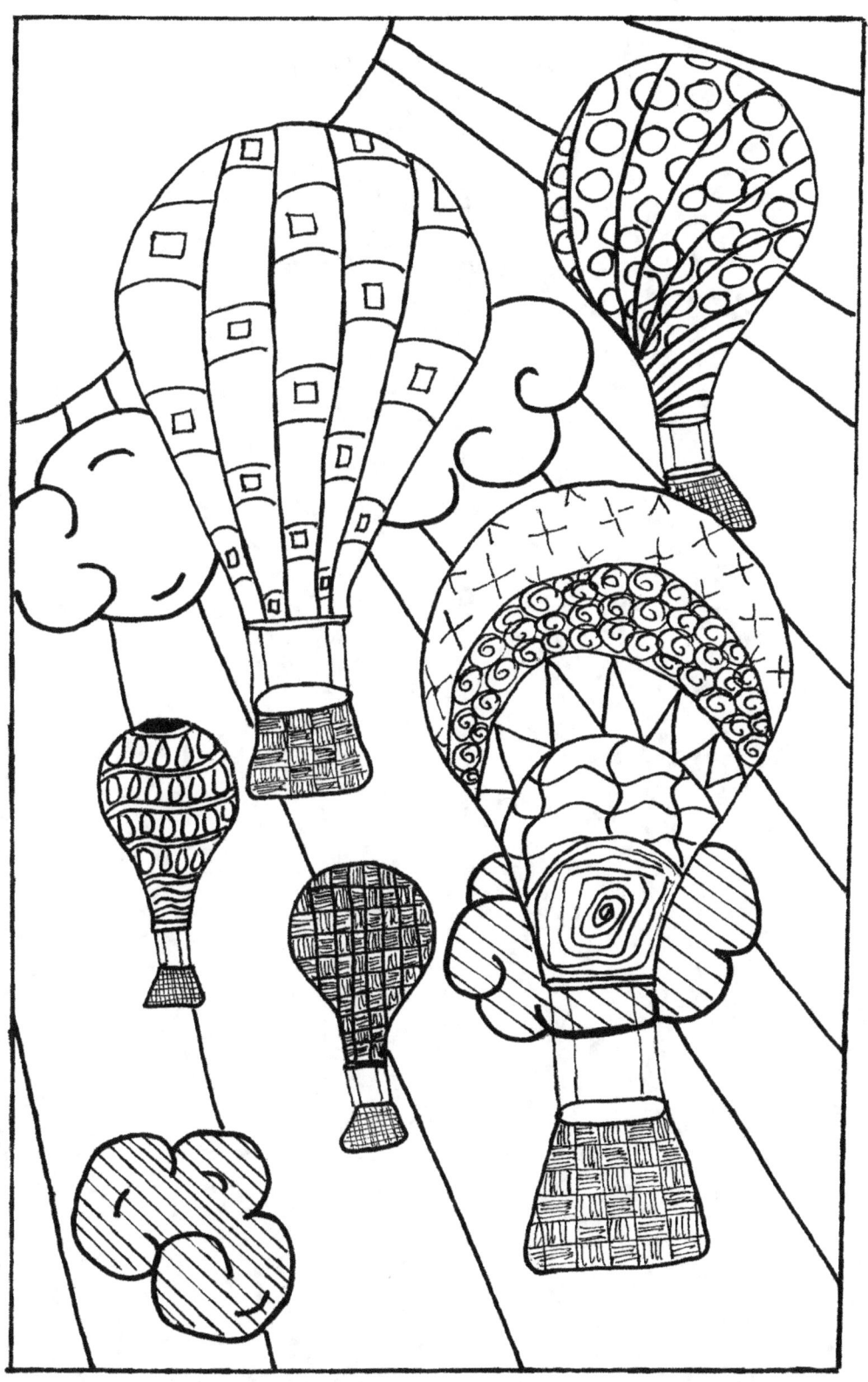

*Contributing Artist*
*Tammy Stansbery*
*USA*

Facebook : TJsArtCorner

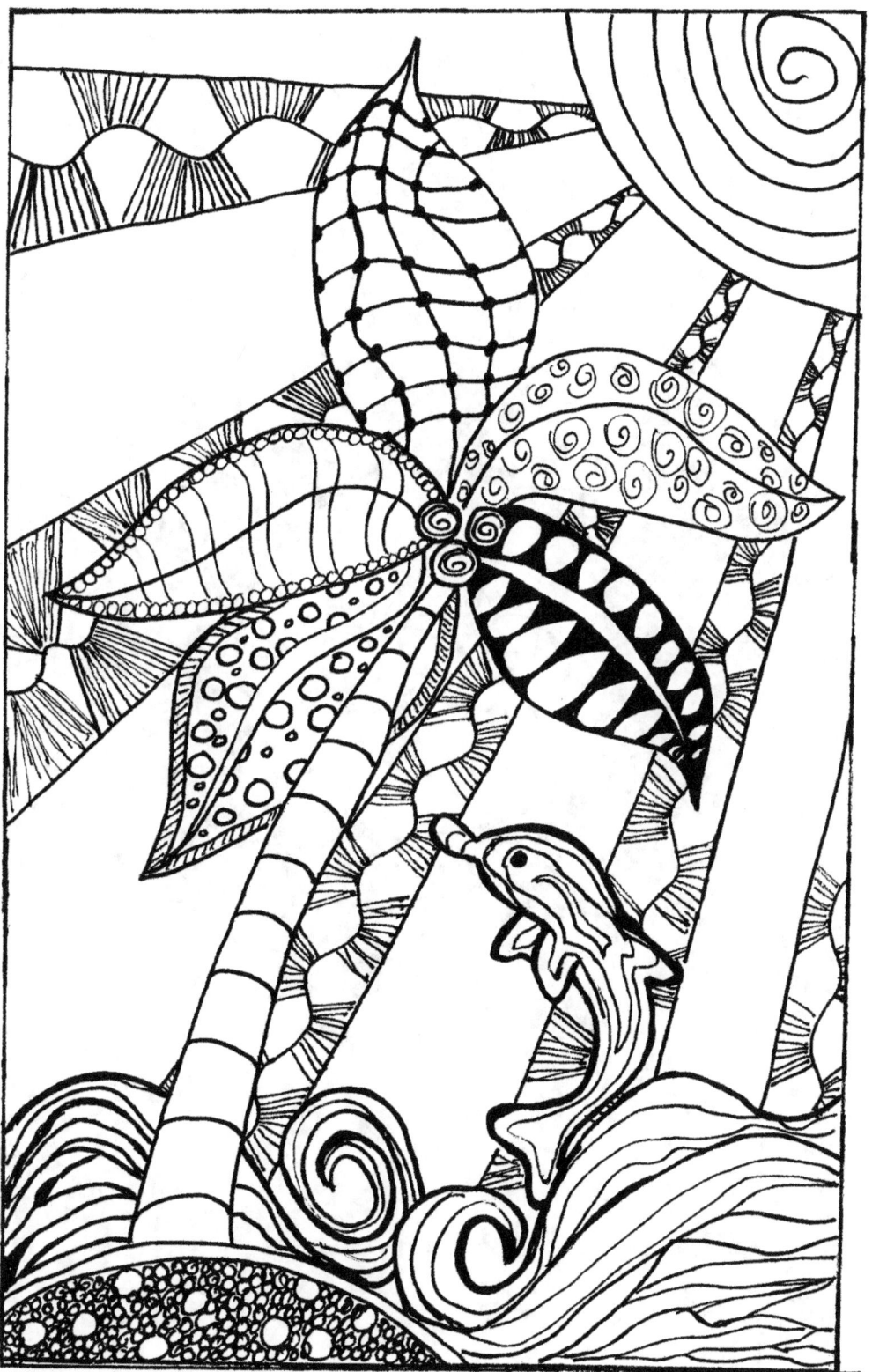

# Backcover
## Drawn & Colored by DomDomx

Published by
"GDG"
Global Doodle Gems

www.ingramcontent.com/pod-product-compliance
Lightning Source LLC
Chambersburg PA
CBHW050115230526
45470CB00004B/1843